POLYDOXY

POLYDOXY

EXPLORATIONS
IN A
PHILOSOPHY
OF LIBERAL
RELIGION

ALVIN J. REINES

Prometheus Books
Buffalo, New York

BL
99
$\cdot R45$
1987
$cop. 2$

90 89 88 87   4 3 2 1

Library of Congress Cataloging-in-Publication Data

Reines, Alvin J., 1926-
    Polydoxy: explorations in a philosophy of
liberal religion.

    Includes bibliographies.
    1. Liberalism (Religion) 2. Reform Judaism.
3. Judaism—20th century. I. Title.
BL99.R45 1987   291'.01   87-2259
ISBN 0-87975-399-4

To Hera, Jennifer, Kip, and Adam
For the present and the future

POLYDOXY

Contents

Preface

In the course of pursuing research for a doctorate, and in my early years of teaching philosophy at a Liberal (Reform) Jewish seminary, I became convinced that a fundamentally new form of religion was in the process of evolving out of the authoritarian orthodox and fundamentalist religions traditional in the Western world. Exploring the nature of this new form of religion has been a lifelong interest of mine.

There have been major indications that a new religious form is emerging. One is the great number of persons who have disaffiliated themselves from their native orthodox and fundamentalist religions in favor of pursuing independent religious choices. Another is the many persons who, despite affiliation with orthodox and fundamentalist religions, reject their authority, and make personal decisions in religious matters. Still another is the existence of various religious structures called "Liberal." Notably these include: Liberal Protestantism, Liberal Catholicism, Liberal Judaism, and Unitarian Universalism. While individuals who reject the authority of the traditional orthodox and fundamentalist religions and the existence of "Liberal" religions point to a new religious form, they themselves provide no clear idea of precisely what this new form is. Even the "Liberal" religions which possess a formal institutional structure fail to present on careful examination a fundamental principle or coherent foundation doctrine. Certainly their communities' beliefs and practices are often vague, generally arbitrary, and frequently self-contradictory.

Upon reflection, I came to the conclusion that "Liberal" religions present a chaotic appearance because they are at a halfway point of development from the orthodox and fundamentalist systems from which they emerged; they therefore exhibit a mélange of bits from the past, pieces from the present, and potentialities for the future. They have not yet reached the new religious form toward which they are tending. The subject of this book is this new religious form that I believe has been in the making.

The purpose of this work is to define this new form of religion, describe its fundamental principles, and explore a number of its ramifications. The name "polydoxy" has been given to this new religious form. Polydoxy is a religious ideology that affirms the ultimate right of an individual to religious self-authority or autonomy; and a religious community that adheres to a polydoxy affirms the ultimate right to religious autonomy of each of its members. Possessed of an ultimate right to autonomy, the individual is free to choose her or his personal religious beliefs and practices, subject only to the limitation that every polydoxian's freedom ends where the other person's freedom begins. Having said this, I leave it to the readers to explore the many details and questions that arise in connection with a polydoxy that this work enters into, from the logical and moral arguments for polydoxy to the definitions of religion and theology that are appropriate to a polydoxy.

I wish to extend my thanks to those who so graciously helped in preparing this book. Melissa Tarkki edited the manuscript with scholarly care. Reverend Jarmo Tarkki studied the work with a critical eye and offered a number of valuable suggestions. Mrs. Betty Finkelstein skillfully and patiently typed and proofread the work in its various stages of development.

My debt of gratitude to my wife, Hera G. Reines, cannot be overstated. She was an active participant in every stage of this work, and meticulously prepared the detailed index that so enhances the text.

Chapter I

Polydoxy and Religious Authority

The philosophy of polydoxy arises from an analysis of the form of authority that is proper for a religion such as Reform Judaism. Accordingly, rather than beginning this work on polydoxy with an abstract, universal treatment of the polydox religious philosophy, it is heuristic to employ Reform Judaism as a concrete example of polydoxy from which the abstract, universal concept will be drawn.

Reform Judaism and Its Analogues

Reform Judaism is the name given to the religion of the Reform Jewish community. The foremost problem confronting the Reform Jewish community at this period of its development is that, although the fact that it exists is clear, what its religion is is not. While it is apparent that the Reform Jewish community is united in its belief that the writings it refers to as its Bible or Scriptures are fallible, its views on other basic subjects, such as the nature of deity, revelation, and the afterlife, are so varied and obscured by disagreement that they cannot be discerned. Accordingly, in the Reform Jewish community, essence (the definition of what Reform is) lags behind existence (the fact that it is), a situation that produces critically serious consequences. For members of a religious community whose religious beliefs are ambiguous and contradictory cannot be expected to attain a coherent religious identity, or the state of authenticity and integrity that such identity brings. The central task of a community such as the

Reform Jewish community, then, is to clarify the essential nature of its religion. The most fundamental of the issues to be resolved in such a clarification of its religion is the concept of religious authority that is proper for it.

The analysis of authority in Reform Judaism to be presented here, however, pertains not only to Reform but also to religions that will be referred to as its analogues. In the nineteenth century, there began to emerge various religious communities that inclined toward the view that the writings they regarded as their Bible or Scriptures were fallible. It is difficult to identify with certainty which religious communities these are since their view that their Scriptures are fallible has not been explicitly stated in their creeds,[1] but left implicit or to the unofficial articulation of individual members. Accordingly, these religions will be referred to in general terms as analogues of Reform Judaism. For example, a Christian religious system that holds its Scriptures, the Old and New Testaments,[2] to be fallible and, therefore, not necessarily true, or a religion that has no Scriptures or infallible truths, is an analogue religion of Reform Judaism. By the same token, a Christian or other religious community that adheres to such an analogue religion is an analogue community of the Reform Jewish community.

The basic meaning of authority, as defined here, is the capacity possessed by some entity, whether a person or group of persons, that enables the entity to compel obedience to its commandments by the person or persons to whom the commandments are issued. An entity can possess authority for one of two fundamental reasons: first, because it has the power, that is, the physical or psychic force, to compel obedience to its commandments; or second, because it has the right, that is, the moral justification, to compel such obedience. The following example taken from the political realm illustrates this distinction. An unlawful government possesses authority over citizens of the country it rules in the sense that it has the power to compel them to obey its commandments, but it does not have authority, in the sense that it has a right, to do so. A lawful government-in-exile, on the other hand, has authority over the citizens of its country in the sense that it has the right to rule them, but it does not have authority in the sense that it has the power.

We may add that, as is evident, it is possible for an entity to possess authority both by right and by power. That is to say, an entity may have both the moral justification to compel obedience to its commandments and the physical or psychic force to do so. In the case of an entity that possesses authority both by right and by power, the fundamental reason that it exercises authority by power is that it possesses authority by right.

The exercise of authority over persons by a community that has the power to do so but not the right is immoral. The reasoning for this assertion is given below. Accordingly, we are not concerned with the question whether the Reform Jewish community and its analogues possess authority by power, but whether they possess authority by right. For inasmuch as they are religious communities, we may presume that they are committed to moral behavior. Consequently, if it can be shown that the Reform community and its analogues do not possess authority by right we may expect that they would neither seek nor exercise authority by power. Since our interest is in authority by right, when the term authority is used without qualification it will henceforth refer to authority by right. Authority by power will continue to be referred to as such.

Absolute and Conditional Authority

For purposes of our inquiry, we will divide the human person into two selves: a *decision-originating self,* a self that creates decisions, and a *decision-executing self,* a self that carries out decisions. Following this distinction, when we say a person is free, we mean that her or his decision-originating self has the authority to enforce the obedience of her or his decision-executing self. When we say that a person is unfree, we mean that some entity external to the person has authority to supersede the person's decision-originating self and to enforce, in its place, the obedience of the person's decision-executing self to commandments that the external entity issues.

We take it to be the case that without reasons to the contrary every person has an ultimate right to be free. Or to translate this statement into terms of authority: every person is presumed, unless reasons are brought forth otherwise, to be her or his own authority, with the right, therefore, to have her or his decision-originating self enforce the obedience of her or his decision-executing self to commandments that she or he issues. This statement is not to be understood as bearing upon the question of whether the human will is ultimately free or determined; it simply means that all persons have the right to determine their own beliefs and actions without external compulsion.

The right persons possess to be free—that is, to be their own authorities—can be acquired by some entity external to the person. When such an acquisition occurs, the entity becomes the person's authority with the right to command the person what to do. The acquisition of the right to authority over a person by an external entity takes place basically in either of two ways. One is by the person voluntarily transferring authority over herself or himself to the external entity; the other is by the external entity coming into possession of such authority in a manner that is independent of the person's consent, and which can be exercised even against the person's will. Authority over a person that is acquired by another entity through the voluntary transfer to the entity of such authority by the person over whom it is exercised is termed *conditional authority*.[3] Authority over a person that is acquired by an external entity independent of the person's consent is termed *absolute authority*. The form of authority with which we are now concerned is absolute authority.

Revelation Authority Argument

Various reasons have been given historically to justify the moral right to absolute authority of familial, political, and religious entities in their respective domains: that is to say, a family leader or council over the individual family member;[4] a political leader or government over the individual subject of the state; or a religious leader, hierarchy, or community over the individual religious community member. Our interest is limited to the third of these, the possession of a moral right to absolute authority over an individual member by a religious leader, hierarchy, or community.

Historically, the prime religious argument for the possession of a moral right to absolute authority by a religious leader or hierarchy has been based upon the theological foundation of a theistic God. By a theistic God is meant a personal supernatural creator and ruler of the universe who reveals to humankind what he wishes them to believe and do.[5,6] The argument proceeds generally in this fashion.

1. There is a theistic God who has created everything besides himself that exists, namely, the universe and all it contains.
2. By the very act of having created them, the theistic God owns all persons and things, and owning them, therefore, possesses absolute authority over them.
3. The theistic God, consequently, possesses absolute authority over humankind.
4. Exercising his absolute authority, the theistic God through a revelation has issued commandments that humankind in general or some particular religious community must obey.[7]
5. The theistic God, also in this revelation, has delegated elements of his absolute authority to a religious leader, hierarchy, or community as a whole that gives them the right to compel humankind or the individual members of a religious community to obey the theistic God's commandments.
6. Therefore, inasmuch as the religious leader, hierarchy, or community as a whole acts with the absolute authority delegated to them by the theistic God, humankind or the individual members of the religious community must surrender all or certain portions of self-authority to the leader, hierarchy, or community as a whole, and obey the commandments that issue from them.

The above argument will be referred to as the *revelation authority argument*. Two elements are clearly necessary to uphold the revelation authority argument: one is the existence of a theistic God; the other is possession of a revelation from the theistic God. If either of these elements is shown not to exist, the revelation authority argument falls. We will now show why the view of revelation necessary to sustain the revelation authority argument does not exist in the Reform Jewish community and its analogues.

Three Forms of Revelation

Revelation may be divided generally into three kinds. The first will be called *verbal revelation;* the second, *ambiguous revelation;* the third, *natural revelation.*

Verbal revelation is defined as a communication from a theistic God to a human mind, a communication of general concepts through words in which equal authority and obligation attach to the literal meaning of the words as to the general concepts they express. Inasmuch as verbal revelation is entirely the product of a theistic God, a being whose mind is perfect, verbal revelation is infallible, wholly without error and incapable of error.

What this means, if the Pentateuch is taken as an example of verbal revelation, is that not only the general concepts expressed in the Pentateuch are binding, but the literal meanings of the words as well. Thus if the Pentateuch states that persons must rest on the Sabbath and are forbidden to do work of any kind,[8] which includes making fire,[9] then not only the general concept that one is not to work must be observed, but the prohibition against making fire must also be literally observed. Hence a person is not free to say, "Making fires in our modern age requires no work at all. Therefore, even if I make a fire and do not keep the letter of the commandment, I am still obeying the Pentateuch so long as I keep the spirit of the commandment and refrain from doing what I consider work." For persons are not permitted simply to keep the spirit or general concept of verbal revelation commandments, the literal meaning of the commandments must be kept as well.

Ambiguous revelation is defined as either the product of a divine influence deriving directly or ultimately from the deity operating upon human faculties, such as reason and the imagination,[10] or the report of a person who has witnessed miracles or other activity issuing directly or ultimately from a deity.[11] Accordingly, ambiguous revelation is in part the result of natural human efforts, and in part the result of divine activity.

What this means, if the Pentateuch is now taken as an example of ambiguous revelation, is that a portion of the Pentateuch results from a deity, and the other portion is human in origin. Consequently, since only a portion of the Pentateuch is conceived of as divine, subsequent generations may in principle discard those parts they consider to be human, erroneous, and historically conditioned, while retaining the parts judged to be divine, true, and timeless. Here, then, a person would be free to accept the general concept of the Pentateuch that one must not work on the Sabbath and reject as archaic the particular rule against making fire that the Pentateuch prescribes. It is even conceivable that new rituals could be created in which the concept of Sabbath rest is more meaningfully expressed.

The critical point must be noted, however, that revelation conceived of as ambiguous is completely fallible in practice. For even though part of the revelation is considered to derive from a deity, and in theory, consequently, is infallible, the determination of which part is divine and which part human is dependent upon the judgment of persons living in later times. Inasmuch as such human judgment is the product of finite minds and inevitably fallible, the content of an ambiguous revelation that is chosen by one person as divine can always be rejected by another who judges it to be human. Accordingly, although ambiguous revelation may be partially infallible in theory, it is entirely fallible in application and practice. If the Pentateuch is taken as ambiguous revelation, how does one know which parts are divine? A person may believe, in fact, that the entire concept of the Sabbath itself is human in origin, and that there is no divine imperative to keep a Sabbath at all.[12]

Natural revelation is defined as that which has been produced by human minds in their search through history for truth, value, and soteria.[13] If the Pentateuch is taken as an example of natural revelation, its concepts and words may be rejected at will, for they are the products of finite, human minds, and, as such, entirely fallible and nonobligatory. Unlike ambiguous revelation, no part of natural revelation is produced supernaturally; it is, therefore, even in theory, entirely fallible, its notions subject to change and development as humans wish. Thus, in practical application, both ambiguous and natural revelation are equally fallible and nonobligatory.

God Views and Forms of Revelation

This discussion regarding revelation has no necessary relevance to the question of God views, for persons who subscribe to different concepts of revelation may still subscribe to similar views on the use of the word God. So we find that persons who hold ambiguous and natural concepts of revelation may at the same time believe in a theistic view of God very much like that of those who accept verbal revelation. One important difference among these theists would consist in the certainty of their knowledge concerning their God view; for the sureness of their knowledge of the existence and attributes of a theistic God is dependent upon the degree of certainty afforded by their concepts of revelation through which such knowledge is attained. Those who accept the concept of verbal revelation would believe their theistic God view to be certain inasmuch as verbal revelation provides infallible knowledge. Those who accept ambiguous revelation would be likely to think their theistic God view almost certain in outline, but probable in detail. Those who accept natural revelation could maintain for their God concept no more probability of truth than any other human knowledge based on comparable natural evidence.

Rejection of the Revelation Authority Argument in Reform

The truth of a concept may be affirmed or denied explicitly: by words. When the concept possesses behavioral implications, it may be affirmed or denied implicitly: by practice. The Reform Jewish community, it is easily seen, has rejected the concept of verbal revelation both explicitly and implicitly. We will first take up Reform's explicit rejection of verbal revelation, and then turn to the implicit rejection. As heirs to a particular historical religious literature, that of the Hebrews, Israelites, and Jews,[14] the Reform Jewish community generally regards only the Pentateuch, Prophets, Hagiographa, and Talmud as presenting a claim to be regarded as verbal revelation.[15] Among these writings, the Pentateuch, containing as it does the only account of the Sinaitic revelation, is considered fundamental, so that if the Pentateuch is rejected as verbal revelation, no credible case can be made for the other biblical writings being verbal revelation. As stated earlier, every word of a verbal revelation is regarded as coming from the mind of a perfect theistic God and is, therefore, literally and infallibly true. Accordingly, a verbal revelation may not be rejected in whole or part by human persons, whose minds are admittedly fallible. If human persons, therefore, should declare that they possess the right to reject whichever parts they choose of a writing that purports to be a verbal revelation, and to judge for themselves what in the writing is true and relevant, then they have clearly repudiated the view that the writing is verbal revelation. Such repudiation of the Pentateuch as verbal revelation is precisely what the Central Conference of American Rabbis has explicitly set forth in a declaration of principles on the nature of Reform Judaism,[16] as the following passages from the declaration testify:

> . . . We hold that the modern discoveries of scientific researches in the domain of nature and history are not antagonistic to the doctrines of Judaism, the Bible reflecting the primitive ideas of its own age, and at times clothing its conception of Divine Providence and Justice dealing with man in miraculous narratives. . . .

> We recognize in the Mosaic legislation a system of training the
> Jewish people for its mission during its national life in Palestine,
> and today we accept as binding only its moral laws, and maintain
> only such ceremonies as elevate and sanctify our lives, but reject all
> such as are not adapted to the views and habits of modern
> civilization. . . .
>
> We hold that all such Mosaic and rabbinical laws as regulate diet,
> priestly purity, and dress originated in ages and under the influence
> of ideas entirely foreign to our present mental and spiritual state.
> They fail to impress the modern Jew with a spirit of priestly
> holiness; their observance in our days is apt rather to obstruct than
> to further modern spiritual elevation.[17]

The Reform Jewish community's implicit rejection of the
concept of verbal revelation is evident from even the most
cursory examination of its ritual and holiday practices. For if the
Pentateuch is believed to be literally true, then one believes that
the commandments it lays down have come directly from a
theistic God and must be obeyed exactly as they have been
commanded. Yet in their observances, Reform Jews uniformly
(and in their opinion, rightly) reject in whole or in part the
practices mandated by the Pentateuch. Consequently, since acceptance of the concept of verbal revelation requires observing
the practices commanded by the Pentateuch, it must be con-
cluded that the Reform Jewish community rejects verbal revelation.

Having, therefore, rejected the concept of verbal revelation,
any documents put forth in the Reform Jewish community as
revelation must be regarded as constituting either ambiguous or
natural revelation and, as such, are fallible.

Returning to our original issue, the crucial question must
now be raised: Can any person or group of persons within the
Reform Jewish community or its analogues, on the basis of
fallible knowledge, justifiably claim to possess absolute authority?
Can they morally choose to lay down commandments that other
members of their communities must obey?[18] The answer is they
cannot. The principle has been laid down that every person is
religiously free, possessing an ultimate right to religious self-

authority. Now, if this principle is to be rebutted by any members of a religious community, they must demonstrate that they possess absolute authority, namely, a right to authority over the other members superior to the latter's own right to authority over themselves. The only way in which members who wish to exercise authority in a religious community can demonstrate possession of this superior right is to show that they have received the right from a theistic God.[19] Members of the Reform Jewish community and its analogues, however, owing to their rejection of verbal revelation, cannot demonstrate that they possess such a right, and must therefore reject the revelation authority argument. Individual members of the Reform community and its analogues over whom the exercise of authority is attempted can always argue that the ostensibly revelatory text upon which those wishing to exercise authority base their claim does not come from the theistic God. And this argument cannot be refuted on the basis of ambiguous or natural revelation, the only forms of revelation to which the Reform community and its analogues can lay claim. Consequently, individual members of the Reform community and its analogues retain their ultimate right to autonomy; seeing that no one in these communities possesses the morally justified absolute authority necessary to enforce obedience upon them.

Absolute Authority Principle: Orthodox Religions

What is the basic organizational principle of religious communities in which every member possesses this ultimate right of religious autonomy? What, in other words, is the basic principle that defines the interpersonal relations among the members of a religious community in which every person possesses the right of self-authority?

This question poses a fundamental problem new to the annals of religion. For religious communities traditionally have been organized on the basis of what may be termed the *Absolute Authority Principle*. The Absolute Authority Principle states that the right exists in a religious community for a member or group of members to exercise absolute religious authority over the other members of the community. Religious communities that believe in the Absolute Authority Principle will be referred to as *authoritarian religious communities;* religions that prescribe belief in the Absolute Authority Principle will be termed *authoritarian religions.* Religious communities historically have been authoritarian and their basic interpersonal structure has been one of leader or leaders to compulsorily obedient followers.

It is significant to note that authoritarian religions historically have also been orthodox religions.[20] An orthodox religion is defined as a religion that asserts as a fundamental principle the belief that there exists an entity, whether deity, deity's viceroy, or otherwise, who not only possesses absolute authority but who has also laid down dogmas and practices that the adherents of the religion must follow. Religions that are both authoritarian and orthodox will henceforth be referred to simply as *orthodox religions,* and similarly, religious communities that believe in religions that are both authoritarian and orthodox will be termed *orthodox religious communities.*

The Absolute Authority Principle to which orthodox communities subscribe opposes religious self-authority. Individual members of orthodox communities are not allowed to determine for themselves the beliefs and practices they will follow. Members of an orthodox community have a duty to obey the orthodox authority, and they possess only those rights granted by or derived from the authority. Accordingly, orthodox religious communities have historically taken the form of totalitarian societies in which autocratic leaders, who have claimed to receive their absolute authority from a theistic deity, have dictated to the members of their communities the beliefs and practices they must follow.

Freedom Covenant Principle: Freedom Covenant Religions

Having explored the nature of the orthodox community, we return to our original question. What is the basic organizational principle of a religious community in which every member possesses an ultimate right to religious self-authority? The principle required must preserve the ultimate self-authority of individual members while at the same time bring them into a communal relationship with one another. The answer I give is the *Freedom Covenant Principle* (or simply, the *Freedom Covenant*). The Freedom Covenant, as I define it, states that every member of a religious community possesses an ultimate right to religious self-authority, and that every member of the religious community pledges to affirm the ultimate religious self-authority of all other members in return for their pledge to affirm her or his own. The corollary of the Freedom Covenant is that the freedom of each member of the community ends where the other members' freedom begins.

The Freedom Covenant and its corollary establish the basic interpersonal rights and duties of the members of the religious community that subscribe to it. Every member possesses an ultimate right to religious self-authority, but, at the same time, has the duty to limit her or his exercise of freedom within the boundary set by the freedom of other members. Thus the Freedom Covenant, in addition to establishing the autonomy of the individual, also establishes a community in which persons enter into a profound and significant relationship of mutual affirmation. Religions to which the Freedom Covenant is fundamental are termed *Freedom Covenant religions;* and religious communities that profess the Freedom Covenant are termed *Freedom Covenant religious communities.*

Another name for a Freedom Covenant religion is *polydoxy,*[21] which literally means "many beliefs." Adherents of a polydoxy may hold different beliefs regarding the various subjects with which religion historically has dealt, such as revelation, immortality, and the meaning of the word God.[22] Thus polydoxies contrast sharply with orthodox religions, for every orthodoxy requires its adherents to hold essentially the same belief regarding a given subject of religion. A religious community whose religion is a polydoxy is termed a "polydox community."

Latent Polydoxy and De Facto Polydoxy

In a polydox community, each member's right to religious autonomy is taken as innate and ultimate; the community consequently has no right to abolish or diminish it.[23] The beliefs and
practices of a polydox community cannot be determined by a
majority vote: No minority, even a minority of one, can be kept
from exercising self-authority. The sole obligation that a polydox
community has a right to demand of its members is observance
of the Freedom Covenant, for this is what each of them has
voluntarily pledged to do.

Having defined the terms polydoxy and polydox community,
it is necessary to introduce four new terms to characterize precisely religions such as Reform Judaism and its analogues. These
terms are necessary because Reform and its analogues generally
do not state expressly that they are polydoxies. Hence language
is necessary to describe religions, religious communities, and persons that are implicitly polydox but have not declared this fact
explicitly. These terms are: *latent polydoxy, latent polydox community, de facto polydox community,* and *de facto polydox
religionist (polydoxian).*

1. A *latent polydoxy* is a religion that does not explicitly affirm
   the Freedom Covenant principle, but which does explicitly
   assert beliefs that contradict fundamental elements of the
   revelation argument for authority and, therefore, of necessity
   denies the argument's validity. One would expect such a religion to commit itself to the Freedom Covenant principle on
   logical and moral grounds, yet the commitment is not explicitly made.
2. A *latent polydox community* is a religious community that
   professes a latent polydox religion.
3. A *de facto polydox community* is a religious community that
   does not declare itself to be a polydoxy, but whose members,
   without expulsion, excommunication, or other disciplinary
   action, behave as if they were adherents of polydoxy, fol-

lowing whatever religious beliefs and practices they choose. A de facto polydox community can be either a latent polydox community or an orthodox community. That is to say, the official or apparent religion of the community is a latent polydoxy or an orthodoxy, but its members' behavior is indistinguishable from that of persons belonging to a polydox community.

4. A *de facto polydox religionist* is one who does not explicitly profess belief in a polydoxy or belong to a religious community that explicitly affirms a polydoxy, but who behaves as a polydoxian, following whatever religious beliefs or practices she or he wishes while tacitly accepting the right of others to do the same. A de facto polydoxian can be a member of a latent polydox community, an orthodox religious community, or belong to no religious community at all.

Given the above classification, we are able to describe with a fair degree of precision Reform Judaism, the Reform Jewish community, and Reform Jews. Reform Judaism is a latent polydoxy. The Reform Jewish community is a latent as well as a de facto polydox community; and Reform Jews subscribe to a latent polydoxy and are themselves de facto polydoxians.[24]

Why Polydoxies Are Not Recognized as Such

Why did not the founders of Reform Judaism openly declare that its adherents possess religious autonomy? The following reasons for the failure of Reform's founders to recognize the polydox nature of their religion extends beyond Reform Judaism, for the conditions they point to still exist and apply, *mutatis mutandis,* to the analogues of Reform Judaism that arose and continue to arise from historical contexts similar to that of Reform.[25]

1. The Reform Jewish community emerged from the Orthodox Jewish community. This close genetic relationship imparted

to the founders of Reform an orthodox model for their own
community, and misled them into thinking of Reform as a
revised orthodoxy.

2. Practically speaking, all other religions of the Western world
were orthodoxies, a fact which made it appear that "ortho-
doxness" was an intrinsic characteristic of religion, and that a
system of belief and practice, consequently, had to be orthodox in order to be a religion.

3. The great figures of the Hebrew, Israelite, and Jewish past,
notably the preexilic prophets, whose teachings regarding
social justice were particularly influential in the early Reform
community, were all authoritarian. Identification with these
prophetic figures by Reform's founders and early leaders
added support to an orthodox interpretation of Reform.

4. Reform's founders and early leaders did not attempt to form-
ulate a synoptic philosophy of Reform that would include
and integrate into a consistent whole its adherents' diverse
beliefs, practices, and critical approach to Scripture.[26] Such
an effort would undoubtedly have pointed to the fact that
only a polydox philosophy could provide the basic principles
necessary to harmonize the Reform community's evident
contradictions in its beliefs, liturgy, ritual, and practices.

Polydox Leadership

One final question remains to be dealt with in this exploration of
authority in polydoxy. What kind of religious leadership is appropriate to a polydox community?[27] Once again polydoxy confronts us with a novel problem. Religious communities historically have been orthodox, and the nature of orthodox leadership is authoritarian. In a polydox community, however, the
notion that any entity possesses absolute authority over other
members is rejected.[28] Moreover, the only ultimate form of
authority that is recognized is each member's self-authority. Accordingly, the sole source of authority in a polydox community
is the self-authority of its individual members. Consequently, if

there is to be leadership in a polydox community that exercises authority over other members such authority must be derived from the self-authority of those members of the community. Since each member has an ultimate right to do with her or his self-authority what she or he wishes, the way in which one member can attain the authority to exercise leadership over other members is for the latter to transfer authority voluntarily to the leader from her or his self-authority. Such authority, in contradistinction to the absolute authority of the leader in an orthodox community, is conditional authority.[29]

The only authority that a member of a polydox community can transfer to the community leader is that which she or he possesses. No member, or group of members, although a majority, can therefore transfer to the leader authority over a member who declines to transfer to the leader authority over herself or himself.

Ordinarily, however, the members of a polydox community will all agree to transfer to the community leader such elements of authority as contribute to the efficacy of the community in fulfilling its fundamental purposes. These include the right to impart factual information or express personal moral opinions to the community at large, to conduct appropriate services, and to officiate at life history ceremonials and rituals.[30]

The word "leader" employed in the above discussion is clearly infelicitous to describe a person who exercises authority in a polydox community, inasmuch as every member is fundamentally her or his own leader, and the nature of the "leader's" authority is conditional upon the individual member's continuing consent. The limitations of conventional language as noted earlier are responsible for employing the term "leader." Thus an apt name that might be put forth to describe a person who exercises authority in a polydox community is *Delegate General.* For the one who exercises authority is an agent to whom authority for specific functions has been delegated by the general membership.[31]

Notes

1. Because Reform Judaism explicitly states that its Scriptures are fallible, it serves especially well as a paradigm for the analysis of religious authority that is given here.

2. Jews employ the terms "Bible" or "Scriptures" to refer to the Pentateuch, Prophets, and Hagiographa; Christians use the term "Old Testament" to refer to these writings. Generally, the term Bible will be employed in this work.

3. Inasmuch as the authority can be attained only on condition that the person over whom the authority is exercised has consented to the transfer.

4. Cf. author's essay, "A Polydox Philosophy of Religious Education," *Polydoxy*, 5, No. 1.

5. The masculine pronoun is used to refer to this concept of the theistic God because it is the general usage in religions that subscribe to this concept of deity.

6. There are many different views regarding the meaning of the word God; see author's essay, "The Word God," *Polydoxy*, 4, No. 1. The "theistic God" includes both the concepts of theistic absolutism and theistic finitism. Theistic absolutism refers to a personal God of unlimited power, and theistic finitism to a personal God of limited power; see pp. 55-7, 73, and cf. 174, 176 ff.

7. Such as the alleged revelations through Moses, Jesus, and Muhammad contained respectively in the Pentateuch, New Testament, and Koran.

8. Exodus 20:10; 31:14,15; 35:2; et al.

9. Exodus 35:3.

10. As, e.g., in Moses Maimonides' view of prophecy; see my *Maimonides and Abrabanel on Prophecy* (Cincinnati: Hebrew Union College Press, 1970), pp. 118-123.

11. As in Martin Buber's view of revelation; cf. M. S. Friedman, *Martin Buber* (Chicago, 1955), pp. 243 f.

12. For a view of Sabbath different from that of the Pentateuch, see my "Shabbath As a State of Being," *Central Conference of American Rabbis Journal* (N.Y., January 1967), pp. 37 f.; also, *Two Concepts of Shabbat*, Institute of Creative Judaism (Cincinnati, 1986).

13. For definition of *soteria*, see p. 63.

14. On the word *Jew*, see *Polydoxy*, 3, No. 1.

15. Orthodox and fundamentalist Christians, however, generally recognize the Bible as being inerrant, but as having been fulfilled and transcended by the New Testament. Muslims also generally recognize the Bible as having been inerrant, but as having been superseded by the Koran.

16. The Central Conference of American Rabbis (CCAR) is the association of rabbis of the Reform Jewish community.

17. Declaration of Principles, paragraph 2, Central Conference of American Rabbis, 1885, *The Jewish Encyclopedia,* 1903 ed., s.v. "Conferences, Rabbinic." The declaration of principles in which these passages appear has come to be known as the "Pittsburgh Platform," after the city in which the Conference was held that issued the declaration.

18. Or anyone else, for that matter.

19. See pp. 16 f.

20. Logically, authoritarian religions need not be orthodox. It is possible to conceive of an authoritarian religious community where those who possess the right to exercise absolute authority over the other members choose not to do so. I am not aware, however, of any authoritarian religion where this has been the case.

21. The term *polydoxy* refers to a Freedom Covenant religion, and is therefore equivalent to the phrase *polydox religion.* When the term *orthodoxy* is used without qualification in this work, it refers to an orthodox religion, although in general usage there are, of course, other orthodoxies than orthodox religions.

22. Since no other term existed, the term *polydoxy* was coined by the author to express precisely this meaning. The word appears in the Greek but with no special technical meaning.

23. In other words, the community affirms and recognizes the individual's right to autonomy, but it does not create it.

24. This same classification applies to the analogues of Reform Judaism, such as Reconstructionist Judaism and the various Protestant denominations that are generally termed "liberal."

25. Arguments can be put forth for any number of dates as the one on which Reform Judaism came into being. We will take 1885 as the formal date of the founding of Reform Judaism, the year in which the Pittsburgh Platform of the Central Conference of American Rabbis appeared; see pp. 21 f. and n. 17.

26. In particular, the critical view that the Pentateuch is fallible, which destroys the foundation of the revelation authority argument.

27. The term "leadership" has meanings and nuances that are unsuitable to a polydoxy but the limits of language necessitate its use until a new term is suggested at the conclusion of the discussion.

28. See pp. 24 ff.

29. See p. 16. One sub-category of conditional authority that deserves mention is *epistemic authority.* Epistemic authority is authority exercised by a person by virtue of being an expert on some subject. A claim to "expertness" does not, of course, give a human person a right to exercise absolute authority over others. One may, however, wish to transfer authority over oneself to some person because the person is believed to be an expert.

30. Life history rituals and ceremonials are those that are observed at the beginning of each new stage of existence and at death.

31. Some traditional names for those who exercise religious authority can be understood in a way that is consistent with the sense of the term Delegate General. The word *rabbi*, e.g., can mean "my teacher." Thus a Delegate General who serves as someone who imparts information can appropriately be called *rabbi*. Similarly, *minister* has the sense of "one who serves." Thus a Delegate General who serves the community can also properly be called "minister."

Chapter II

Liberal Religion: Orthodox and Polydox

In the course of the collective history of humankind as well as the individual history of the human person, terms often come into use before they have received conscious attention and deliberate definition. The history of philosophy and religion is testimony to this point. One of the more difficult tasks for those who must deal with such terms is to recognize that despite their familiar sound they have no generally accepted or precise definition, and as such cannot be employed in disciplined discourse without first having received the degree of meaning necessary for technical communication. "Liberal religion" is, I believe, among the terms that have entered into common use without adequate definition having been afforded them. The following is an analysis of the term liberal religion that offers a clarification of its use from the polydox point of view.

A basic point to be made with respect to the name *liberal religion* is that the term *liberal* is part of it. This term comes from the Latin *liber,* meaning free. Consequently, we may assume at the outset that a liberal religion is one that in some special sense gives its adherents freedom. Based on the kinds of freedom that religions which have been called liberal have given their adherents, there are two major categories of liberal religion, *polydox* and *orthodox,* with orthodox liberal religion further dividing into two subcategories, *supernatural orthodox liberal religion* and *natural orthodox liberal religion.* Our discussion will begin with a description of polydox liberal religion, for it is only after understanding the nature of polydox liberal religion that the meaning of orthodox liberal religion becomes clear.

Polydox Liberal Religion

Polydox liberal religion is equivalent to polydoxy which, as defined earlier, is a religion that affirms the Freedom Covenant. The Freedom Covenant states that every adherent possesses an ultimate right to religious self-authority, and the freedom, consequently, to believe and practice as she or he chooses so long as there is no infringement upon the rights of others.[1] The freedom a polydoxy permits its adherents is the maximum possible for persons who live in an organized community and possess the ultimate right to self-authority; the freedom of each necessarily limits the freedom of the others. One creedal principle must be affirmed by polydoxians in order to attain the maximum freedom possible—the Freedom Covenant. Without this single dogma, there cannot be a maximum freedom religion that is subscribed to by more than one person, that is, by a community of persons. In brief, a polydox liberal religion is synonymous with a polydoxy, and it provides its adherents with the greatest degree of freedom possible for a religion professed by autonomous adherents who are in a community relationship with one another.

Orthodox Liberal Religions

Liberal religions other than polydoxies limit the creedal freedom of their adherents, and impose dogmas beyond that which is logically or organizationally necessary for a maximum freedom liberal religious community. For this reason, these liberal religions are here termed orthodox.

Two categories of orthodox liberal religions can be distinguished: *supernatural* and *natural.* Orthodox supernatural liberal religions are orthodox liberal religions in which the dogmas required include beliefs in supernatural entities or beliefs and practices that are obligatory for some supernatural reason. Orthodox natural liberal religions are liberal religions in which the dogmas laid down consist entirely of beliefs in natural entities or refer to acts that are obligatory solely for natural reasons. We will first take up orthodox supernatural liberal religions.

Orthodox Supernatural Liberal Religions

Three kinds of orthodox supernatural liberal religions are commonly referred to: *Liberal Catholicism, Liberal Protestantism,* and *Liberal Judaism.* There exists, to the author's knowledge, no formal definitions of these three kinds of liberal religion. Still, from the literature in which they are referred to, broad characteristics of each can be discerned:

1. Liberal Catholicism: the religion of persons who reject or regard as nonessential (and, therefore, unobligatory) any part of the traditional Roman Catholic doctrine or practice mandated by the Pope and Roman Catholic hierarchy,[2] but who accept as true and valid all remaining traditional Roman Catholic doctrine and practices, which, accordingly, constitute their religion.[3] Typically, Liberal Catholic dogmas include some form of divine status for Jesus and special status for the authority of the Pope and Church teachings.[4]
2. Liberal Protestantism: the religion of persons who affirm intellectual liberty and the spiritual and ethical content of Christianity but also lay down dogmas that assert some form of divine status for Jesus and usually for the New Testament as well.[5,6]
3. Liberal Judaism: the religion of persons who affirm intellectual liberty and reject the infallibility of the Bible but generally lay down as dogmas the existence of a theistic God, the unique covenantal and providential relation between this theistic God and Jews, and divine status of some kind for the Bible.[7,8]

Orthodox Natural Liberal Religions

The adherents of orthodox natural liberal religions who belong to organized religious groups are most often found in the societies of the Unitarian Universalist Association, the Ethical Culture

Movement, and some Quaker groups. It is likely, however, that there are numbers of such adherents to be found in traditional religious communities and others who belong to no organized religious community at all.

Among the dogmas typically laid down by orthodox natural liberal religionists are the following:[9]

1. Liberal religionists must affirm the right of persons to freedom of religious belief.[10]
2. Liberal religionists must accept rationalism, that is, they must base their beliefs on reason.[11]
3. Liberal religionists must accept empiricism, that is, they must harmonize their beliefs with experience as understood by science.[12]
4. An authentic liberal religionist does not believe in a theistic God or supernatural powers.[13]
5. Liberal religion is opposed to solitary and contemplative religion.[14]
6. According to liberal religionists, theists are not religious, only pantheists are; that is, persons are religious who "recognize themselves as part of the Life Force" and "if they feel as part of the universe." This is the "great truth and inspiration of Liberal Religion."[15]
7. A liberal religionist believes in the perfectibility of humankind.[16] "Man is a creature," says Argow, "of infinite capacity who is capable of making come true the ancient dream of a kingdom of heaven upon the earth."[17] Opton declares similarly that liberal religion "promises to create . . . the Kingdom of God on earth."[18]

Why Orthodox Liberal Religions
Are Called Liberal Religions

The question immediately comes to mind why in the course of history orthodox supernatural and natural liberal religions ever came to be named "liberal," given the fact that liberal means "free," and these religions, by imposing dogmas upon their adherents, certainly do not provide them with a free religion. Can rational justification be offered for the use of the name *liberal,* or is it simply a historical misnomer? The answer, upon analysis, is that rational justification can be given, but we will find that the name is given to orthodox supernatural liberal religions and orthodox natural liberal religions for different reasons.

Why Orthodox Supernatural Liberal Religions
Are Called Liberal Religions

As defined earlier, an orthodox religion is one that lays down dogmas and obligatory practices that the adherents of the religion must follow.[19] In orthodoxies such as Roman Catholicism, the various Prostestant denominations, and Orthodox Judaism, numerous supernatural dogmas are laid down.[20] There appear at times within the institutions or communities of the orthodoxies persons who, while retaining membership in the institutions and communities, nonetheless maintain that only part, not all, of the dogmas these orthodoxies lay down are, in fact, dogmas and as such require belief. In other words, these partial dissenters reject some dogmas established by the orthodoxies to which they ostensibly adhere, but they retain others. These remaining dogmas are declared by the partial dissenters to constitute the true and proper form of the orthodoxy.

The partial dissenters come to be called liberals and their religion liberalism. The reason for this can now be made clear. Dogmas incumbent upon a person restrict that person's freedom. Accordingly, the fewer the dogmas, the greater the freedom. Consequently, the version of an orthodoxy that prescribes fewer dogmas restricts its adherents' freedom less than the original orthodoxy, and is, therefore, termed liberal, that is, free in contrast to the original. Hence Liberal Catholicism puts forth fewer dogmas than does regular Catholicism, and consequently allows its adherents more freedom. Similarly, Liberal Protestantism and Liberal Judaism require fewer dogmas than the original orthodox forms from which they are carved, and likewise they allow their adherents more feedom.

The point must be emphasized, however, that orthodox supernatural religions are true orthodox religions, and as such differ fundamentally from polydox liberal religions. No orthodox supernatural liberal religion asserts the basic right of the human person to ultimate religious freedom, and all would deny in practice, if not in words, the fundamental principle of polydox liberal religion that every person possesses a right to ultimate religious self-authority. If adherents of an orthodox supernatural religion reject its dogmas and mandatory practices, they are regarded as sinners or heretics, and they are subjected to whatever punishment the community has the power to enforce.[21]

Why Orthodox Natural Liberal Religions
Are Called Liberal Religions

We come next to the question why orthodox natural liberal religions have been named liberal in view of the many dogmas they prescribe. That these dogmas go far beyond that which is justifiable for a true liberal religion which affords maximum freedom is clear from an analysis of the dogmas typical of orthodox natural religions enumerated above.[22]

The first dogma is that liberal religionists must affirm the right of their adherents to freedom of religious belief. No fault can be found with this from the viewpoint of a true liberal religion except that it is immediately contradicted by the dogmas that follow.

The second dogma is that liberal religionists must affirm rationalism and base their beliefs on reason.[23] If, however, according to the first dogma, liberal religionists have a right to freedom of belief, what right does one liberal religionist have to dictate to others how they shall arrive at their beliefs? What sound reason can be given to prohibit persons from basing their religious beliefs upon will, emotion, imagination, or on whatever basis they choose?[24]

The third dogma is similar to the second and objectionable in the same way. What conceivable justification can a religion that affirms an individual's freedom of religious belief have to demand that its adherents arrive at their beliefs on the basis of empirical experience as understood by science?[25] Why should not persons who possess religious freedom be allowed to fashion their religious beliefs from whatever realm of psychic experience they wish? Any number of ultimate interpretations of phenomena different from or outside the conceptions of science can be given,[26] and it makes no moral sense to forbid someone doing so.

The fourth dogma, which denies a liberal religionist the right to believe in theism or supernaturalism, profoundly violates a person's autonomy. It is quite difficult to understand how any religion that claims to provide its adherents with religious freedom can deny them the right to believe as they will with respect to the term deity and the existence of supernatural powers.

The fifth dogma asserts the right of the orthodox natural liberal religion to determine for its adherents the way they must understand the term religion. There are many different definitions of the term, and it is an essential element of religious freedom that persons have the right to determine for themselves what their definition of religion is.[27]

The sixth dogma, in effect, declares that an orthodox natural liberal religion has the right to determine what religiousness is, and what kind of deity (pantheistic) one must experience to be accounted religious. It is difficult to see how such orthodox natural liberal religion is significantly less restrictive than orthodox religions have been historically. Moreover, the sixth dogma, in addition to subverting the first dogma, also contradicts the second and the third dogmas. Nothing in empiricism or science allows us to speak of the existence of a "Life Force." Furthermore, from the point of view of empiricism and science, feeling oneself "as part of the universe" surely must be accounted a fantasy.

Like the sixth dogma, the seventh contradicts the first, second, and third dogmas. It is difficult to conceive of a requirement more invasive of religious privacy than that one must believe in the "perfectibility of man," and that liberal religion will create "the Kingdom of God on earth." Certainly, such a belief cannot be substantiated by reason, empirical experience, or by science.[28]

Three reasons are prominent among those that can be given why natural orthodox liberal religions have been called "liberal" despite the numerous dogmas they mandate.

First, orthodox natural liberal religions generally state explicitly that they believe in the religious freedom of the individual. Few enough persons, adherents or otherwise, then look beyond this avowal of freedom to the additional dogmas laid down that contradict the initial declaration of individual religious autonomy.[29]

Second, orthodox natural liberal religions reject the supernatural dogmas of the traditional orthodox religions as well as the dogmas of the orthodox supernatural liberal religions. To many persons, accustomed to the restrictions on freedom of these supernatural religions, "real" dogmas are supernatural dogmas—natural dogmas are not perceived as dogmas. Consequently, the dogmas of orthodox natural liberal religions, which are natural, are not recognized as dogmas, and orthodox natural liberal religions are taken as "liberal."

Third, orthodox natural liberal religions frequently refer to themselves as liberal religions. When coupled with the two preceding points, this self-designation, albeit literally inaccurate, has come into general use largely undisputed.

Polydoxy Differs from Orthodox Natural and Supernatural Liberal Religions

Comparing orthodox natural liberal religions with polydox liberal religion, there is one element they both share in common. Each explicitly affirms the principle that its adherents possess a right to exercise individual religious autonomy, which polydoxy frames in terms of the Freedom Covenant. Where they differ is that polydoxy allows no additional dogmas, for the simple reason that any additional dogma would contradict the Freedom Covenant. According to polydoxy, orthodox natural liberal religion is liberal only in the sense that it provides its adherents with freedom from the obligation to accept supernatural religious dogmas. It must be stressed, however, that orthodox natural liberal religions do not provide their adherents with the pure liberal religion that a polydoxy does, in which persons are freed from both supernatural and natural dogmas.

Polydox liberal religion is, then, essentially different from both orthodox supernatural liberal religion and orthodox natural religion. The difference is based on principle. Polydoxians believe that no religious community has moral justification for compelling its adherents to accept more than the one dogma of the Freedom Covenant. As discussed earlier in detail, polydoxians believe that only a religious community that possesses a verbal revelation from a creator god of the universe that grants some member or group the right to exercise absolute authority over other members can give a religious community the authority to compel its members to accept dogmas.[30] Since polydoxians contend that no credible evidence for such a revelation exists, no religious community, therefore, has a right to lay down any dogmas other than the Freedom Covenant. For without a verbal revelation, every person has a right to self-authority, and the one way in which this right can be assured is through the Freedom Covenant.

Differences among Polydoxies

Religions are constituted of both essential beliefs and practices, which will be referred to as *essentials*,[31] and nonessential beliefs and practices, which will be referred to as *nonessentials*. The essentials of a religion are those beliefs and practices that are constitutive of the religion and which a person, therefore, must accept in order to be an adherent of the religion. The nonessentials of a religion are those beliefs and practices that are not constitutive of the religion and which a person, consequently, can reject yet still remain an adherent of the religion.[32] Religions that have different essentials are different religions and are said to differ *essentially*. Religions that share the same essentials, whether or not they have different nonessentials are essentially similar, that is, they constitute the same religion. Religions that are essentially similar, but whose nonessentials differ, are said to differ *nonessentially*.

All polydox religions are essentially the same in that they share the same essential: the dogma of the Freedom Covenant. Yet we can speak of different polydox religions in that polydoxies can differ from one another nonessentially. Polydoxies can differ nonessentially by having different names, symbols, liturgies, and holidays. Polydox religions fall into two broad categories: particular polydoxies and universal polydoxies.

Particular Polydoxies

Particular polydoxies are the religions of polydox communities that employ particular nonessentials, that is, nonessentials such as names, symbols, liturgy, and holidays, that for cultural or historical reasons are meaningful to some polydoxians but are meaningless or have negative value to others. Although those nonessentials may be themselves entirely undogmatic—they neither state nor imply that those who use them believe or profess some theological creed or doctrine—they can still be felt by some polydoxians to be inappropriate for their use. An example of a particular nonessential is the name "Jew." A person who has the name Jew does not by virtue of that fact believe in some particular religious dogma or necessarily in any dogma at all. Historical and contemporary experience and usage show that the name Jew has no one meaning. Some polydoxians, then, choose to refer to themselves as Polydox Jews because the name Jew has nonessential significance for them but in no way contradicts their basic commitment to polydoxy.[33] Still, despite the fact that the name Jew is only a nonessential and consistent with essential polydox belief, there are nonetheless polydoxians who by virtue of their personal history do not identify with the name and do not find it relevant to their religious expression. It goes without saying that inasmuch as the name Jew is a nonessential, both Jewish and non-Jewish polydoxians, whatever their particular name or other nonessentials may be, follow the same religion, polydoxy, for they all affirm as the essence of their faith one principle: the Freedom Covenant.

One may add that names such as "Christian" and "Humanist," among others, have had a history similar to the name "Jew." That is to say, they have no single or intrinsic meaning, and persons who employ them as their religious names do not thereby necessarily signify some particular religious or theological dogma.[34] Accordingly, there are polydoxians who have the name "Polydox Christian" as there are others who have the name "Polydox Humanist."

Universal Polydoxies

Universal polydoxies are the religions of polydox communities that employ no particular nonessentials, such as names, symbols, liturgies, or holidays that for cultural or historical reasons are associated with some specific group, and are, therefore, relevant to some polydoxians but not to others. A member of a universal polydox community might simply call her or himself "Polydoxian" or "Polydox Adherent," rather than a Polydox Jew or Polydox Christian. The holidays of a universal polydoxy are entirely different from those of traditional Jewish and Christian celebrations, employing neither their names, forms, or dates.[35] The neutrality of the universal polydoxies, namely, the fact that their nonessentials are undogmatic and bear no relation to the cultural or historical observances of particular polydoxies, enables all polydoxians in principle to participate in them. The universal polydoxies serve not only those who eschew particularism, but also provide a meeting place where the members of particular polydoxies can come together to experience in common the Freedom Covenant essence they share together.

A Comparison of Polydoxy and Orthodoxy

The nature of polydoxy is perhaps most clearly revealed by comparing it with traditional orthodox religion.[36] This comparison serves to point up the significant differences that exist between polydoxy and orthodoxy.[37] It is understandable that these differences can give rise to psychic, cultural, and semantic barriers that obstruct the recognition that polydoxy is a religion. For until very recently, orthodoxy alone was regarded as "religion" by almost everyone. Nevertheless, by confronting the matter directly, one can hope that the resulting familiarization will dissipate polydoxy's novelty and overcome whatever resistance there is to recognizing it as another religious form.

1. A polydox community is created by the act of humans. When a group of persons enters into a Freedom Covenant with one another for the purpose of religious expression, a polydox community comes into existence. It is unnecessary, of course, for a community or its members to take the name "polydox"; a polydox community has the right to choose for itself whatever name it pleases. The community is polydox provided that its members are mutual participants in a Freedom Covenant.

   Orthodox communities understand themselves to have been established supernaturally by a theistic deity. Thus Orthodox Jews maintain their community was founded by the covenant the Hebrews made with the god Yahveh at Mt. Sinai; Roman Catholics claim their community was founded by Jesus; and Muslims assert their community was founded by Allah through the intermediation of Muhammad.

2. The creed and single dogma of a polydox community, the Freedom Covenant, claims no more for itself than that a group of humans arrived at the judgment that it is true and morally valid, and chose, therefore, to conduct their lives in accordance with it.[38] As the product of the finite human mind, the judgment that the polydox creed is true is admittedly fallible.

Each Orthodox community claims that its particular creed was revealed by an absolute theistic deity. Accordingly, since the author of the creed is unconditionally perfect, the creed is necessarily true and infallible.[39] No refutation of the creed is possible, and no new knowledge will ever appear that will contradict it.

3. Every member of a polydox community is his or her own religious leader; that is, every member is autonomous. There is no person in the community who has the authority to command or prescribe to others except by their invitation and consent.

In orthodoxy, the community is governed by religious leaders who claim to possess authority to prescribe to their fellow members (or to humankind at large), with or without their consent, what they must believe and how they must behave. Thus members of orthodox communities must surrender their autonomy to the communities' leaders. These leaders maintain that authority is theirs by divine right; that is, it comes from a theistic deity and not from humans, and cannot, therefore, be taken away by humans. Hence Orthodox leaders base their authority on verbal revelation, either a revelation that some other person has received and from whom the leader and community receives through tradition,[40] or a revelation the leaders have personally received.

4. No services, rituals, or ceremonies are obligatory in a polydox community. Each person determines individually whether to keep observances, and what form these observances will take. In short, all observances in a polydox community are non-essentials.

In an orthodox community, there are usually a great number of observances that every member must keep. These observances are dictated by the community's religious leaders, who, in turn, generally claim they were commanded by a theistic god.

5. Instruction in a polydox community can be used to educate, but not to *endoctrine*.[41] By education is meant imparting

information in such a way that the student has the capacity to judge the truth or falsity of the information critically and objectively. Thus education requires, among other things, imparting accurate and unprejudiced information, presenting all sides of an issue, and the creation of a learning environment in which the information imparted can be accepted or rejected without fear of punishment, psychological or physical. Endoctrining is the opposite of education. Endoctrining is the imparting of partisan information in a manner and an environment both of which are calculated to persuade the student to accept uncritically the information given. The Freedom Covenant prohibits endoctrining, for endoctrining takes away a person's ability to make a free decision, thereby violating the person's right to autonomy.

The usual method of instruction in an orthodox community is endoctrining. Use of endoctrining is justified on the basis that the information imparted is infallible knowledge from a perfect theistic deity. Accordingly, to give students the opportunity to reject such absolute knowledge is simply to invite them to acquire and hold erroneous beliefs.

Concrete Polydox Communities

One final point remains to be explored with respect to polydoxy: this is to illustrate the manner in which a concrete polydox community is structured. We will examine first a particular polydox community and then turn to a universal polydox community.

A Concrete Particular Polydox Community

The concrete particular polydox community we will look at is a Polydox Jewish community.[42] A Polydox Jewish community is brought into existence when a group of persons who possess the name Jew enters into the Freedom Covenant relationship with one another and decides the following: to call the community so formed *Polydox Jewish;*[43] to name the religion of the community

Polydox Judaism; and to name the members of the community *Polydox Jews.*[44] The way in which a person becomes a Polydox Jew is by joining the Polydox Jewish community and in this way signifying affirmation of the Freedom Covenant, the choice to take the name Polydox Jew, and the desire to call her or his religion Polydox Judaism.

Hence once a person becomes a Polydox Jew, her or his religion is known as Polydox Judaism. Any given Polydox Jew's Judaism consists of two elements, the essential and nonessential. The essential element consists of the Freedom Covenant, to which all polydoxians subscribe; the nonessential element consists of those beliefs and practices superadded to the essence that individual polydoxians may follow as they wish. As indicated earlier, nonessentials might include personal morality, beliefs regarding the word "God," and holiday observances.

In light of the above, care must be taken to distinguish among three possible meanings of the term Polydox Judaism. Polydox Judaism may refer to its essence, the Freedom Covenant, to which every Polydox Jew adheres; to the entire religious system of some individual Polydox Jew, which includes both the essence, namely, the Freedom Covenant, and whatever nonessentials the individual may subscribe to in addition; or to the aggregate of individual Polydox Jewish systems, that is, the totality of different systems to which the entire community of Polydox Jews subscribes. We can distinguish among these three meanings where necessary by referring to the first as *essential Polydox Judaism,* to the second as *individual Polydox Judaism,* and to the third as *aggregate Polydox Judaism.*

The point must be emphasized that every individual Polydox Judaism is valid. Although individual Polydox Judaisms may contain contradictory nonessentials—for example, they may have different views of the word "God"—both are properly referred to as Polydox Judaism, and those who profess them are equally authentic members of the Polydox Jewish community.[45] So long as the Freedom Covenant is affirmed, it does not matter how opposed individual Polydox Judaisms are in their nonessentials, they are all valid systems of aggregate Polydox Judaism.

Reform Judaism

A Polydox Judaism, like other polydox communities, need not call itself by the name "Polydox."[46] There are, for example, many Reform Jews who consider Reform Judaism to be a polydoxy.[47] Taken as a polydoxy, Reform is structured in the following way. Affiliation or membership is employed to determine who is a Reform Jew. Affiliation with the Reform community performs two functions: it symbolizes acceptance of the Freedom Covenant, and it gives to the affiliated the name Reform Jew, after the community of which they are members. The Reform Jewish Community is constituted of these formal institutions: the Central Conference of American Rabbis (CCAR), the Reform rabbinic association; the Union of American Hebrew Congregations (UAHC), the primarily North American Reform congregational association; and the Hebrew Union College-Jewish Institute of Religion (HUC-JIR), the Reform rabbinic seminary. Following the affiliation definition, a Reform Jew is a person who is a member either of the CCAR, of a congregation associated with the UAHC, or the HUC-JIR student body.[48]

Inasmuch as the constitutive factor in being a Reform Jew is affiliation, which symbolizes affirmation of the Freedom Covenant, every Reform Jew possesses the right to accept whatever nonessentials she or he wishes. Consequently, since Reform Jews have the right to choose whatever nonessentials they please, all nonessential beliefs and practices they choose are Reform Jewish,[49] and the entirety of an individual Reform Jew's essential and nonessential beliefs and practices constitute an individual Reform Jewish system. Thus the term Reform Judaism, like the term Polydox Judaism, can possess three different meanings. Reform Judaism can refer to the Freedom Covenant affirmed by all Reform Jews explicitly or implicitly; Reform Judaism can refer to the personal system of an individual Reform Jew; and Reform Judaism can refer to the aggregate of individual systems subscribed to by the totality of Reform Jews. When necessary, these three meanings can be distinguished in the manner set forth for Polydox Judaism, by referring to the first as *essential Reform Judaism,* to the second as *individual Reform Judaism,* and to the third as *aggregate Reform Judaism.*

Concrete Universal Polydox Communities

Polydox Judaism, Polydox Reform Judaism, and Polydox Christianity are all terms that refer to particular polydoxies. A universal polydoxy, in contrast, employs no particular nonessentials, such as names or holidays, that are meaningful to some polydoxians but not to others. Accordingly, a universal polydoxy is established when a group of polydoxians enter into a Freedom Covenant relationship with one another, and choose as the names and practices of the group nonessentials that all polydoxians can find meaningful. The point should be made that although a universal polydoxy does not as a group employ particular nonessentials, this does not bar individual members from doing so personally, as, for example, referring to themselves as Polydox Jews or Polydox Christians. Thus a universal polydoxy provides a community to which Polydox Jews, Christians, Hindus, Humanists, and all other polydoxians can belong without imposing their cultural or historical preferences upon one another. For in the universal polydox community all names held in common and all observances practiced in common are neutral with respect to such particularity. This is seen in the one concrete universal polydox community that has been established, the Polydox Confederation. To the Polydox Confederation, all members are polydoxians, and no particular nonessentials are employed.

Notes

1. See pp. 24 f.
2. Such rejection has historically brought condemnation. J. H. Newman writes: "Liberalism then is the mistake of subjecting to human judgment those revealed doctrines which are in their nature beyond and independent

of it, and of claiming to determine on intrinsic grounds the truth and value
of propositions which rest for their reception simply on the external authority of the Divine Word" (*Apologia Pro Vita Sua* [New York, 1968], p. 218).

3. This description accords with the definition of "Liberal Catholic"
given in *Webster's New International Dictionary of the English Language*,
2nd ed. (1954), s.v. "Liberal Catholic," "A person or group of persons
rejecting the authority of the Roman Catholic Church in specific matters of
doctrine, discipline, and church government, but accepting the body of its
teachings, its forms of worship, or the like. . . ."

4. Special in the sense that it is not the status that regular Catholics
accept, seeing that Liberal Catholics feel that the authority of the Pope and
Church teachings can be set aside at times.

5. By "divine status" for the New Testament is meant that it is supernaturally revealed or inspired in some way but does not constitute verbal or
infallible literal revelation. Fundamentalist Protestants, in contrast, believe
the New Testament constitutes verbal revelation.

6. It is Liberal Protestantism as here described by the name "orthodox
supernatural liberal religion" to which W. P. Roberts refers in the following
statements: "I maintain that Liberal Protestantism, Liberal Christianity, is
not anti-dogmatic, is not anti-theological"; and, "Now I am positively for
dogma, and so I am sure is every Liberal Christian" (*Liberalism in Religion*
[1886], pp. 56 and 59). Similarly, D. E. Miller writes: "If one elects to be
part of the Christian community, then one does not live on the purely
pragmatic plane; one lives 'in God' and 'through Christ'—however this experience may be symbolized in one's consciousness" (*The Case for Liberal
Christianity* [San Francisco, 1981], p. 66).

7. By the Bible (i.e., Pentateuch, Prophets, Hagiographa) having "divine status of some kind" is meant that it is revealed or inspired but does not
constitute verbal revelation. Thus the Bible in Liberal Judaism has a status
similar to that of the New Testament in Liberal Protestantism.

8. A typical expresssion of Liberal Judaism is the *Union Prayer Book*
(Cincinnati, 1936). The term Liberal Judaism is at times used to refer to
both orthodox supernatural liberal religious belief and Jewish polydox
belief, but generally it refers only to the former, and is so used in this work.

9. It is of interest to note that orthodox natural liberal religionists are
generally averse to calling the mandatory beliefs they lay down by the names
"creed" or "dogma," no matter how dogmatic they may be. W. A. Argow
writes: "Because of their arbitrary presumptions the great definitive creeds
of early Christianity have small place in the philosophy of the liberal . . . .
The liberal holds the creeds are fumbling, childlike answers fashioned in a
prescientific era. Instead he prefers to give his allegiance to certain immut-
able principles . . . 'The brotherhood of man,' 'the perfectibility of man,' 'the
superiority of reason to superstition and unreason,' . . . These are principles,
not dogmas or creeds" (*What Do Religious Liberals Believe?* [The Antioch
Press, 1950], pp. 16 f). Given ordinary dictionary usage the mandatory and

fundamental beliefs Argow and other orthodox natural liberal religionists lay down are dogmas, and they are referred to as such here.

10. Argow, *op. cit.,* pp. 16 f.; F. G. Opton, *Liberal Religion* (Buffalo, 1981).

11. Argow, *ibid.,* pp. 17 f.; Opton, *ibid.,* pp. 89 ff.

12. Argow, *ibid.,* p. 19; Opton, *ibid.,* pp. 89, 107, 110.

13. Argow, *ibid.,* p. 19; Opton, *ibid.,* pp. 38, 49, 85.

14. Opton, *ibid.,* p. 31.

15. Opton, *ibid.,* p. 38; cf. Argow, *op. cit.,* p. 30.

16. Argow, *ibid.,* pp. 17, 35; Opton, *ibid.,* p. 23.

17. *Ibid.,* p. 26.

18. *Op. cit.,* p. 12.

19. See p. 24.

20. The term *orthodoxy* will be used to refer to orthodox religions in the usual sense; liberal orthodoxies (Liberal Catholicism, etc.) will be referred to as orthodox liberal religions.

21. It is unnecessary for our purposes here to enter into the question whether communities that subscribe to orthodox supernatural liberal religions have a moral right to exercise authority over their members. It all depends whether their beliefs will support the revelation argument for a moral right to absolute authority, which requires belief in a verbal revelation, pp. 18 f. above. Cf. the ratio-moral authority principle, p. 122.

22. P. 36.

23. There is a disturbing technical naiveté and lack of critical thinking that appears to permeate much of orthodox natural liberal religious writing. For one thing, the assumption appears to be made that rationalism has some one meaning and that all who base their beliefs on reason will come to the same conclusion. Those who are acquainted with the history of philosophy are aware of the falsity of this notion. Rationalists have disagreed with one another on just about everything, including what is meant by rational. One need only think of three famous rationalists: Descartes, Spinoza, and Leibniz.

24. As stated above (n. 21) with respect to orthodox supernatural liberal religion, it is unnecessary to go into the question whether advocates of orthodox natural liberal religions have a moral right to dictate to other members of their community. Suffice it to say that from a polydox viewpoint they do not. For, by definition, adherents of orthodox natural liberal religion reject belief in verbal revelation, which is necessary to support the revelation argument for a moral right to absolute authority, the only ethically acceptable argument for absolute authority that exists. Orthodox natural liberal religionists believe only in natural events whereas verbal revelation is a supernatural communication miraculously created by a theistic deity.

25. The same technical naiveté that natural orthodox liberal religions show with respect to rationalism and reason appears with respect to science. Science is treated as if it were a unified, harmonious, and certain body of

knowledge that is definitive and decisive for religious belief. This is a misunderstanding of science, and scientists would be the first to say so. In point of fact, science has nothing definitive or decisive to say about any given religious belief, from views of the deity to revelation and the afterlife.

26. Metaphysical interpretations, for example, can provide for some adherents an attractive basis.

27. The author's definition of *religion* is presented in Chapter III.

28. It is puzzling how any ideology based on empiricism and science could arrive at such conceptions as "the perfectibility of man" and the ability of humans through natural means to attain the "Kingdom of God." Apparently, these notions come as a reaction to opposite notions in traditional Christian belief. Adherents of orthodox natural liberal religions often seem to feel that true religious belief is the very opposite of that which traditional religion teaches is true. Another possibility exists, namely, neither that which a traditional religion teaches nor its opposite is true.

29. One liberal religionist who is aware of the inconsistencies and ambiguities in orthodox natural liberal religious teaching simply accepts it as inevitable, reflecting "the human condition" (Opton, *op. cit.,* p. 25). Such contradictions are, of course, not the inevitable result of the human condition, considering that polydox liberal religion eliminates them.

30. See pp. 16 f.

31. The totality of a religion's essentials constitutes its essence; see pp. 41 f. and 96 ff. A polydoxy's essence consists of one essential, the Freedom Covenant.

32. In Orthodox Judaism, for example, the daily prayers prescribed for men are not obligatory upon women. Thus these prayers are essentials for the men, but nonessentials for the women, who may recite them or not, as they choose. For examples of Catholic nonessential beliefs, see pp. 142 f.

33. The name Jew, for example, can have value as an ontal symbol to Polydox Jews in a way that it would not have for a polydoxian who by virtue of birth and cultural semantics received the name Christian. By the same token, the name Christian could under similar conditions have the value of an ontal symbol. For ontal symbol, see pp. 166 f.

34. In the course of history, "Christians" have subscribed to all varieties of theological belief, from theism to nontheism and from supernaturalism to naturalism. Similarly, the term "humanist" has enjoyed a variety of meanings: from those who are theists and supernaturalists who stress human concerns to those who reject all theological language and stress the human individual's capacity for self-realization through reason.

35. To illustrate: whereas in the spring, Polydox Jews might celebrate a polydox Passover on the date determined by the traditional Jewish calendar, and Polydox Christians might celebrate a polydox Easter on the date determined by traditional Christian calculation, universal polydoxians in the spring could celebrate a holiday such as the Festival of Creative Freedom on the vernal equinox.

36. Such as is represented by Orthodox Judaism and Roman Catholicism, *not* orthodox liberal religion.

37. A further comparison between Polydox Judaism and Roman Catholicism appears on p. 151 in the distinction between modernist Judaism and Catholicism.

38. This is the only claim for which there is objective evidence. Individual polydoxians can subjectively claim whatever private evidence they wish, including personal revelation.

39. Each orthodox community has a different and mutually exclusive creed which means that if one is true, the others are false. Accordingly, every orthodox community claims that its creed is true and the others are in error. Unfortunately, no orthodox community offers a method whereby it can be demonstrated objectively to a neutral observer that its creed alone is true and all others are false.

40. Usually the original person who receives the revelation is said to have lived in some much earlier time, as, e.g., Moses or the disciples of Jesus.

41. For further discussion of education and endoctrining see *Polydoxy, A Polydox Philosophy of Religious Education,* Vol. 5, No. 1, p. 4. As stated there: "Endoctrining" is employed as a technical term. The meaning is similar in a general way to one sense of the term "indoctrination," which is, however, too loose for the precise use desired here.

42. A Polydox Christian community, or any other concrete particular polydox community would, *mutatis mutandis,* be structured in the same way.

43. Other terms can replace *Polydox,* such as *Creative* or *Reform* (see below), but the terms *Jew* and *Jewish* are constants.

44. The question arises: by what right does a group of Jews use the term *Judaism* for Polydox Judaism, seeing that the term already appears in the name Orthodox Judaism, which is a different religion from Polydox Judaism. There are a number of different (but complementary) answers of which two will suffice here. First, no present Jewish religious community originated the term *Jew,* and no present Judaism is the original religion to which the name Judaism applied. Second, the practice for over two millennia has been for Jewish religious communities to appropriate the names Jew and Judaism for their own use from preceding Jewish communities. Thus Pharisaic Judaism took the name from Sadducean Judaism, and Reform Judaism from Orthodox Judaism. Many other examples of this practice can be given of which Polydox Judaism is simply among the latest.

45. Because beliefs in Polydox Judaism are nonessential, and therefore optional, Polydox Judaism eliminates the bitter heresy conflicts that have always beset orthodox religions, where beliefs are essential.

46. See above, n. 43.

47. The difficulty in dealing with Reform Judaism is that it has never been formally defined: one might say the definition of Reform is in process. As stated earlier, there is no question that Reform is a latent polydoxy (p.

27), but since it has not been formally defined, one is hesitant to say it is an actual polydoxy. Nevertheless, many Reform Jews consider their religion an actual polydoxy, and that's how this book will describe it. For further discussion of Reform Judaism as a polydoxy, see the author's article "Reform Judaism," *Meet the American Jew*, ed. B. Menkus (Nashville, 1963), pp. 29 ff.

48. The faculty and staff of the HUC-JIR, however, are employees rather than members of an ideological community.

49. To deny Reform Jewish status to these nonessentials is to deny those who follow them the freedom they have under the Freedom Covenant.

Chapter III

A Definition of Religion

Importance of a Definition of Religion

The word "religion" has no single or absolute meaning, and in the course of history it has received a variety of definitions. This point is of great practical as well as theoretical importance. For a person may reject "religion" defined one way as meaningless, and refuse membership in the religious community that subscribes to "religion" so defined, whereas the same person will gladly belong to another community that defines "religion" in another way. This fact is particularly important in view of the present, precarious state of organized religion in the Western world. There can be little doubt in the mind of the objective observer that, taken as a whole, the dominant religious institutions of the scientifically, technologically, and industrially advanced societies of the Western world are declining. While the purpose of this inquiry is primarily a theoretical one, to offer a new definition of the word religion, a new definition has fundamental practical consequences. For in the author's view, among the primary reasons for the deteriorating condition of Western religious institutions is the definition of "religion" to which they subscribe. As now defined by the dominant Western religious institutions, "religion" refers to beliefs and emotions that ever greater numbers of persons either do not have or which they find unrealistic and irrelevant to their lives. Yet the word religion can be defined in a way that it is competent for the modern age.

This point may be enlarged on as follows:

1. The definition of the word religion to which a religious institution subscribes determines the institution's essential focus,
purpose, and activity. To illustrate: the nature of a medical
institution is determined by its definition of the word "medicine"; so that a medical institution that defines "medicine" as
"supernatural faith healing" will employ procedures and practices which an institution that defines "medicine" in scientific
and natural terms will reject. Likewise, religious institutions
whose definitions of "religion" differ will pursue dissimilar
goals and activities.

2. The definition of "religion" to which the presently dominant
Western religious institutions subscribe, either explicitly or
implicitly, is "belief in God," in which the term "God" is
understood as *theistic absolutism*. Theistic absolutism is a
concept of God according to which the word God refers to an
omnipotent, omniscient, omnibenevolent, miracle-working being who created the human race and all the universe, who
revealed to humankind commandments it must obey, and
who, depending upon its obedience, dispenses to humankind
supernatural rewards and punishments both in this world and
in a hereafter.

3. Having thus defined "religion" as "belief in theistic absolutism," Western religious institutions direct all their activities,
liturgical, ritual, and educational, to the single, ultimate purpose of serving the concept of theistic absolutism. The liturgies of these institutions consist of praises of, pledges of obedience to, and protestations of total dependence on the deity as
conceived in theistic absolutism. The rituals of these institutions relate all natural and personal experience to the theistic
absolutistic deity. And religious education consists primarily
in efforts to propagandize the congregation, particularly the
young, with a blind belief in theistic absolutism, along with
an unquestioning loyalty to the institution which usually presents itself as divinely and uniquely "Chosen."

It may be taken as evident—if only from the great numbers
of persons who choose to be unaffiliated with religious insti-

tutions, and the very large numbers of those affiliated who do not participate in religious activities—that despite the considerable cultural visibility and political strength of the institutions that espouse theistic absolutism, the importance of the theistic absolutistic view of deity is steadily diminishing in modern life. (One need only glance at the history of the Middle Ages to see what societies that take theistic absolutism seriously do look like.) Accordingly, it can be expected that the presently dominant religious institutions of society, based as they are on religion defined as "belief in theistic absolutism," will continue their decline, perhaps to the point of dissolution. Thus it is not too much to say that the future of organized religion in Western society depends upon the development and institutionalization of a definition of religion that is broader and deeper than the restrictive and limited "belief in theistic absolutism."

Polydoxy as a Source of a New Definition of Religion

Whence is a new definition of religion to come? It is certainly unreasonable to expect such creative innovation from the traditional theistic absolutistic religions of the Western world, Orthodox Judaism, Roman Catholic Christianity, Islam, fundamentalist Protestantism, and their externally similar modernistic outgrowths such as traditionoid[1] Reform Judaism and Liberal Protestantism. These institutions share a vested interest in propagating the view that "belief in theistic absolutism" is the only true definition of religion. Theistic absolutism, their primary dogma, is part of their essence. If these institutions are able to preserve and spread the view that the only proper definition of religion is "belief in the theistic absolutism" (along with the related misconception that theistic absolutism is the only correct meaning of the word God), they can then perpetuate the myth that this belief is necessary to religion. And such a myth supports the position that they alone teach and serve the only true form of religion. Once the word religion is so defined as to include meanings other than "belief in theistic absolutism," however, then the theistic absolutistic religions can no longer claim a monopoly either on the word religion or its practice. If there can be authentic religion without theistic absolutism, there can then be authentic religion that is not Orthodox Judaism, Roman Catholicism, Islam, fundamentalist Protestantism, traditionoid Reform Judaism or Liberal Protestantism, and the like.

It is perhaps here, then, in the development of a new definition of "religion," that polydoxy, aside from its own emergence, has its most important contribution to make to the evolution and history of religion. For a polydoxy, unlike the aforementioned religions, can produce a new definition of "religion." The polydox community possesses the two basic qualifications necessary to the development and institutionalization of a new definition. First, a polydoxy has no vested interest in theistic absolutism as the meaning of the word God. A polydoxy allows all views on the word God, from theosupernaturalism to atheonomatism.[2] Consequently, a definition of religion that includes the option of theistic absolutism, but to which theistic absolutism is nevertheless unessential, is appropriate to a polydoxy. Second, a polydox community affirms the ultimate personal freedom of every member, which includes the right to understand the word religion as the individual deems proper. Such freedom not only releases the creativity necessary to develop a new definition of "religion," but also encourages the institutionalization of the definition, namely, the incorporation and integration of the definition's principles into the liturgical, ritual, and educational materials of the community.

Proceeding, then, with the recognition that the individual members of a polydox community have the right to judge for themselves its merit and relevance to their lives, we turn now to the following discussion in which a new definition of religion will be developed and proposed.

Three Fundamental Features of the Human Person

Before proceeding to the proposed new definition of religion itself, it will be helpful to present a description of three fundamental features of the human person upon which the definition is based. These are: *finity, infinite conation,* and *the conflict between awareness of finity and infinite conation.*

Finity

Finity, as revealed by introspection and observation, is a pervasive feature of the human person. All structures and powers of the human being, psychic and physical, are finite; that is, they come to an end before reaching an ideal state; they always fall short of perfection and self-sufficiency. The human person is a finite being enclosed within a state of imperfection by a limiting boundary. Basic categories of human finity include: *psychic finity, physical finity, territorial finity,* and *existential finity.*

1. *Psychic finity* is exemplified by the intellect and emotions. Both fall short in a striking fashion of attaining an ideal status. Were the human intellect to function in an absolutely perfect way, it would know all there is to know: the past, the present, and the future. It would know why and how the universe and the human person came into existence; it would know all natural laws and humankind's ultimate destiny. As it is, even the greatest of human intellects have acquired only small and partial fragments of knowledge. The human intellect being finite, one cannot know for sure what will take place over the next moment of existence, even whether this moment will occur. Uncertainty and risk are the inevitable consequences of intellectual limits. Similarly, the emotions reveal their finity. Humans lack emotional self-sufficiency, unable by their own power to achieve a state of happiness. A person cannot attain felicitous emotional states in isolation from other humans. Human happiness generally is dependent upon relationships of esteem, affection, or love with other

persons, and particularly must there have been such relationships during the periods of infancy and childhood.

2. *Physical finity* is seen in the senses and the body generally.
   The sense of sight shows well what it would mean for a
   bodily power to function in an absolutely perfect manner.
   Ideally, sight would perceive without error and at one time
   everything in the universe that is visible. Owing to its inherent
   limits, however, sight cannot perceive objects too small or too
   far away; and can apprehend nothing at all with absolute
   certainty of accuracy. The body is the most obvious example
   of the human lack of self-sufficiency. By itself, without air,
   water, or food, the body quickly perishes. Moreover, even if
   its basic needs are satisfied, the body is at all times vulnerable
   to injury and disease, and it is subject to aging.

3. *Territorial finity* is the limit on every human's power to possess things, dominate events, and rule other persons. However
   much wealth and power a person may have, there are always
   possessions, events, and persons beyond control or out of
   reach.

4. *Existential finity* is the inability of the human person to continue in existence, so far as ordinary observation can tell,
   beyond a very limited period of time. The natural consequence of existential finity is death, the most dramatic of all
   instances of finity.

Infinite Conation

The second feature of the human person germane to religion is
infinite conation. ("Conation" is the general philosophic term for
desiring, willing, and the like.) Infinite conation is the intense
willing within humans that wants without limit or end whatever
is conceived or imagined to be pleasurable. Infinite conation is
itself a pervasive or general will that is expressed through particular desires, imparting to them an infinite quality. As might be
expected, the principal categories of particular desires through
which infinite conation is expressed correspond to the general

areas of human finity: psychic desires, physical desires, territorial desires, and existential desire. When infinite conation is expressed through a category of particular desires, these desires themselves become infinite and may be termed: *infinite psychic conation, infinite physical conation, infinite territorial conation,* and *infinite existential conation.*

1. *Infinite psychic conation* includes the desire to know everything knowable with absolute accuracy and certainty. Particularly desired is such metaphysical knowledge as the complete truth about ultimate reality and the meaning of the word God; whether there is a hereafter; and its exact nature if there is one. Also included in infinite psychic conation is a desire for absolute emotional invulnerability and self-sufficiency.
2. *Infinite physical conation* includes the desires for omnipotence and bodily invulnerability. Infinite physical conation can also be expressed through the various bodily appetites, such as sex, for example. Infinite sexual desire is a craving for unbounded libidinal experience without regard for social or reality limits.
3. *Infinite territorial conation* is the desire to own and rule the universe: to possess all things, control all events, and dominate all other persons. Infinite territorial conation may extend to the point where there is not only a desire to own and rule all that there is, but to be all that there is.
4. *Infinite existential conation* is the will to live forever, the desire never to die.

The Conflict of Finitude

The third characteristic of the human person relevant to religion is the conflict produced by human finity and infinite human conation. When existing simultaneously within a person, the awareness that one is finite and the passionate desire to be infinite are mutually incompatible and clashing forces. The human person, bounded and limited, yearns intensely to be what she or he is not, unbounded and unlimited. This conflict between the awareness of one's finity on the one hand, and infinite conation on the other, will be referred to as the *conflict of finitude* or simply as *finitude*. Four basic observations are to be made with respect to the conflict of finitude.

1. The first is that the conflict of finitude takes place on both a conscious and unconscious level. This point is of fundamental importance in attempting to understand and evaluate the conflict of finitude. For to the degree that finitude occurs on an unconscious level, it is not present to consciousness except in a disguised and distorted form. Yet despite the considerable extent to which finitude does reside in the unconscious, a fairly adequate idea of the conflict can be attained by consciousness. For one thing, some aspects of the conflict of finitude are present to consciousness. The most notable of these is the conflict between existential finity and infinite existential conation, between the awareness that one dies and the profound wish not to die. Still, the fact that much of the conflict of finitude takes place in the unconscious produces difficult problems with respect to understanding and recognizing the conflict for what it is.

2. The fundamental point to be made regarding the conflict of finitude is that, unresolved in a person, the conflict annihilates the meaning of existence. The negative moods produced by finitude, such as terror, despair, angst, and melancholy, are so intense that the meaningful aspects of existence are overpowered and life's value corroded. One need only think of the mood generated by the concrete contemplation of one's own death while fervently wishing not to die. Many destructive moods that appear to the consciousness as rootless and without cause are actually attributable to those aspects of the conflict of finitude that take place in the unconscious.

3. The conflict of finitude, from the available evidence, is an inherent problem of the human being. This means the conflict is not produced by some particular culture, economic system,

or political structure, although these entities can influence the severity of the problem and the manner with which it is dealt.

4. Inasmuch as the conflict of finitude is an inherent, universal problem of human existence, the entire structure of the conflict, namely, the awareness of finity, infinite conation, and the conflict itself can appropriately be referred to as the *ontal structure*. ("Ontal" is derived from the Greek word for existence or "being.") The ontal structure behaves much as a single, dynamic structure. When a change takes place in a person's awareness of finity or infinite conation in a way that affects the conflict of finitude in a lasting manner, this is an *ontal change* or a *change in the ontal structure*. The act of insight or will that produces a change in the ontal structure is an *ontal decision*.

Religion: Response to the Conflict of Finitude

The negative moods produced by the conflict of finitude create intolerable psychic pain, and an urgent need, therefore, to deal with the conflict. The way in which a person deals with the conflict of finitude will be referred to as the person's *response to the conflict of finitude,* or briefly, *response to finitude*. With this we have arrived at our definition of religion: *Religion is the human person's response to the conflict of finitude*. Stated more fully: Religion is the human person's response to the psychic conflict produced by the clash between the awareness of finity and infinite conation, the passionate desire not to be finite. The ideal purpose of a religion is to provide a response to the conflict of finitude that enables a person to resolve the conflict and thereby attain a state of ultimate meaningful existence that the conflict's negative moods would otherwise destroy. The state of ultimate meaningful existence that is attained when the conflict of finitude has been resolved will also be referred to as *soteria*.[3]

Thus the function of a religion is to produce soteria. Two other states of being may be counterposed to soteria: *dyssoteria* and *asoteria*. Dyssoteria is the state attained by a partial resolu-

tion of the conflict of finitude; asoteria is the state that arises
from a failure entirely or almost entirely to resolve the conflict.
Persons in a state of dyssoteria find their existences sporadically
meaningless for significant periods of time; those who are in an
asoterial state suffer meaninglessness all or most of the time.

Major Responses to Finitude

There are three major categories of responses to finitude (or
religions): the *infinite response,* the *discognitive response,* and
the *finite response.* In the discussion that follows, the three major
categories will be described and commented upon.

    The conflict of finitude, as described earlier, is produced by
the simultaneous presence within a person of two clashing
psychic forces: awareness that one is finite, and the intense desire
to be infinite. The infinite response resolves the conflict by denying the truth of the notion that the human person is finite, which
removes one of the conflicting psychic forces, and by asserting
that, on the contrary, the human individual is infinite, which
satisfies the other. In this way, with the consciousness of finity
removed, and the wish to be infinite fulfilled, the human's ontal
structure becomes integrated. This integration produces soteria,
the state of ultimate meaningful existence. There are two major
kinds of infinite responses to finitude: the *infinite personal response* and the *infinite relational response.*

Infinite Personal Response to Finitude

The general features of the infinite personal response are the
beliefs that the person is infinite, and that this power of infinite
existence comes from no source other than the person. The person, consequently, is not dependent on any other being for infinity. The common form that the infinite personal response
takes is that the person believes herself or himself to be "God."
God here is usually understood in a pantheistic, acosmic, or
egotheistic sense, and refers to a being who is uncreated and

absolutely independent, illimitable, timeless, omnipotent, and the sole reality. The perception that the human person is finite, according to this view, stems from illusion or partial knowledge.

Another form of the infinite personal response is that the person, though not "God," is nevertheless independently infinite. The way this happens is that the person is conceived of as possessing an uncreated soul or consciousness which is by its nature eternal, so that the person is not dependent upon any other being for infinity.

Infinite Relational Response to Finitude

The infinite relational response holds that human persons, so far as their own powers are concerned, are finite; but they can attain infinite status through a dependent relation on an infinite being, usually, the deity of theistic absolutism, who has the power to grant infinity to others. The classic formulation of the infinite relational response in the Western world was framed by Pharisaic Judaism,[4] and it has been followed in its basic principles by Roman Catholicism, Islam, and fundamentalist Protestantism. The infinite relational response has for some two thousand years been the Western world's basic response to finitude and its primary means of attaining soteria. For this reason, and because it is now becoming increasingly ineffective, the salient aspects of the infinite relational response deserve enumeration.

The cardinal requirement of the infinite relational response to finitude (as of all infinite responses) is that the religionist making the response believes with the profoundest conviction in the existence of the beings and the reality of the events that the infinite relational response presupposes. Genuine belief is required; lip service will not do. Not because lip service is wrong, but because it is ontally (structurally) ineffective. The conflict of finitude exists entirely in the human psyche and can be overcome only by potent psychic actions, that is, by a conviction powerful enough to produce ontal decisions that forge the beliefs and desires of a person into an enduring integrated structure. An allied point, but no less significant, is that the infinite relational response (as is true of all responses to finitude) is ultimately made alone. The human person has a unique and privileged relationship to her or his own existence, so that only the one who has the conflict of finitude possesses the necessary access to the self to resolve it. No one can resolve the conflict for another. No one for another can assent to the beliefs and perform the acts of will that constitute the ontal decisions which resolve the conflict between awareness of finity and infinite conation. This is not to say that philosophers, theologians, depth psychologists, sages of all kinds, and parents cannot provide guidance and support to those who seek help in responding to finitude. Without such assistance there are countless numbers who would never reach the point from which they could then proceed to respond to finitude successfully. It is simply that in the end every person confronts and responds to finitude alone.

The primary belief of which one must be convinced in order to make the infinite relational response of Pharisaism and Western religion generally is that theistic absolutism is true; namely, that there exists an infinitely perfect personal deity who exercises providential care over humankind in this life, that after death this care continues, and that this providential care is now and will be in the future granted the believer. It is understandable from this analysis how "belief in theistic absolutism" has come to be synonymous with "religion" in the Western world. The response to finitude of the dominant religions of the Western world is totally dependent upon belief in theistic absolutism. Also, theistic absolutism pervades Western cultural, educational, political, and economic institutions. Still, the notion that "belief in theistic absolutism" is a competent definition of religion is philosophically and historically inadequate, and fails to reveal the basic nature of "belief in theistic absolutism" as a response to finitude. Accordingly, "belief in theistic absolutism" is not a unique phenomenon, but merely one of several possible responses to finitude. Consequently, as the fundamental and general activity underlying and including the infinite relational response, it is *response to finitude* and not *belief in theistic absolutism* that merits the general name, *religion.*

The Pharisaic Jewish infinite relational response is based on the belief that"God" (as the word is defined in theistic absolutism) supernaturally and infallibly revealed to Moses the commandments that appear in the Pentateuch and Talmud. Without an infallible communication of commandments, there would be no way to know and obey what the "God" of theistic absolutism wants believed or performed, and hence no way to receive the reward of a blissful afterlife. In Christianity, the positions of Moses and the Pentateuch are occupied by Jesus and the New Testament, and in Islam, by Muhammad and the Koran.

It is a subtle but nevertheless significant point to distinguish between the nature of the infinite desire represented by the infinite personal response and that represented by the infinite relational response. In the infinite personal response, the nature of the desire expressed is to be infinite through one's own power, either by possessing an uncreated and immortal soul, or by being "God," absolutely self-sufficient and all that there is, the only reality. In the infinite relational response, the nature of the desire is to exist in perfect security in and through another. That is, the desire is to be not only finite, but to be passive, cared for, and receive infinite existence through a dependent relation to a deity.

As stated above, a person must be genuinely convinced of the truth of the basic beliefs that underlie the infinite relational response for the response to be efficacious and produce soteria. Historically, genuine conviction has been achieved by basing belief on evidence. The ultimate evidence for the Pharisaic infinite relational response is contained in the Pentateuch; for the Christian infinite relational response, in the New Testament; and for the Muslim, in the Koran. Consequently, if the credibility of these three works were to be vitiated, no evidence for the traditional Western infinite relational response would exist. Accordingly, the ability of the infinite relational response to resolve the conflict of finitude in our age depends upon the ability of the Pentateuch, New Testament, and Koran to convince the modern

Western mind that one or all of them is literally and infallibly true. There are persons, it is true, who do not require evidence to support their infinite relational responses. Such responses are, however, subjectively fashioned and objectively baseless responses.

Discognitive Response to Finitude

The discognitive response deals with the conflict between awareness of finity and infinite conation in an essentially different way from the infinite response. The infinite response removes one of the antagonistic forces, awareness of finity, and satisfies the infinite desire that remains. The conflict of finitude is thereby resolved. In the discognitive response, however, the conflict is not resolved; it is concealed. As noted earlier, the conflict of finitude when unresolved produces negative moods that annihilate the meaning of existence and cause unbearable psychic pain. The discognitive response obscures from consciousness either knowledge of the conflict, or knowledge of the intolerable anguish it causes, or both. Among the discognitive responses subscribed to in our time, these are especially prominent: psychosis and neurosis, alcoholism, drug addiction, and suicide.

Several comments on the discognitive response to the conflict of finitude are in order.

The question can be raised why the discognitive responses to finitude are so widespread in our time. There are two points that taken together provide, if not the entire answer, a good part of it. The first is that in our scientific and critical age, ever greater numbers of people simply do not find the evidence necessary to support an infinite response convincingly. It has always been difficult in Western society to believe oneself "God" as is required by the infinite personal response—although some increased acceptance of such notions has taken place with the emergence of various exotic cults. More significant is the fact that only recently have massive numbers of persons in Western society been unable to accept the beliefs required for the infinite relational responses of the traditional Western religions: Orthodox Judaism, Roman

Catholicism, Islam, Protestant Christianity, and their modernistic outgrowths such as traditionoid Reform Judaism. No small part of this disbelief has been created by scientific and critical inquiry into the three works referred to above as constituting the only ostensibly objective evidence that exists for the infinite relational response, the Pentateuch, New Testament, and Koran.[5] The conclusions of such inquiry are invariably that the three works are clearly fallible, of uncertain accuracy, and consequently of no real value as theological evidence. It is ironic that the vast majority of scholars who have come to these conclusions are professors at theological seminaries.

Many other reasons may be cited for the widespread rejection of the infinite response religions,[6] but the point is that such religions are widely rejected and this fact is momentous. For these religions have provided Western civilization with its primary means of achieving soteria. Added to the rejection of the infinite response is the second point, that no other response to finitude that resolves the conflict, such as the finite response to be presented next, is generally known, let alone recognized as a religion, institutionalized in a religious organization, systematically taught, and culturally sanctioned. Accordingly, many modern persons are trapped, unable to subscribe to the traditional infinite responses on the one hand and unaware of or unschooled in any other resolving, soterial response to finitude on the other. Thus beset by the unendurable anguish of the conflict of finitude, they resort to discognitive responses in the hope of concealing at least for the time they can the dyssorterial or asoterial agony that annihilates the meaning of their lives.

The conflict of finitude is most intense during adolescence.[7] We may expect, therefore, that during this period such discognitive responses as drug addiction, alcoholism, and suicide will be particularly widespread.

The discognitive responses cannot be considered authentic responses to finitude, in that they do not resolve the conflict. Such responses only make the person unaware of the conflict: drugs and alcohol numb and fog the mind; suicide kills it. Moreover, except in the case of suicide, the person remains subconsciously or unconsciously aware of the conflict, and great suffering takes place even though diffused or disguised by the illness or chemical employed. The conflict of finitude, until it is properly resolved, is an essential and fundamental part of the human person, so that it is not possible to destroy awareness of the conflict and its pain without destroying the person as well.

Finite Response to Finitude

The third response to the conflict of finitude is the finite response. The finite response contains essentially three elements: acknowledgement of the truth of the perception that one is finite; renunciation of infinite conation; and setting and accepting limits in all areas of desire. Several forms of the finite response occur, based on different views of ultimate reality, and requiring different degrees of renunciation, but all share in common renunciation of infinite existential desire and acceptance of the finality of one's own death. Accordingly, with infinite desire given up, the conflict of finitude, which is produced by the clash between consciousness of finity and infinite desire, is resolved. The finite existence of the human person, consisting of psychic, physical, territorial, and existential limits, satisfies a finite will; the finite being that a person is, is that which the person wishes to be. Consciousness and will having thus been integrated, the harmony brings soteria. A number of observations will serve to deepen understanding of the finite response.

The first relates to the obvious question: how is it possible to renounce infinite conation, accept the finality of one's own death, and still attain soteria, ultimate meaningful existence? As the efficacy of the infinite response for the modern human weakens, the answer takes on fundamental significance for the success and quality of the individual's life in modern society. In the following brief outline, the author's view how the finite response brings soteria is sketched.

1. Ultimate meaningful existence, and all positive moods, such as happiness or contentment, result from the satisfaction of conation, that is, of will or desire.

2. There is in the human person a profound will to exist. The mere act of existing satisfies this desire, so that one's individual existence is in itself intrinsically meaningful since it satisfies a desire flowing from the depths of one's being.

3. If a person's will to exist desires infinite existence, however, the only act of existing, that is, the only form of human existence that will satisfy it is infinite existence. Accordingly, the conflict of finitude arises when a person perceives her or his existence as finite, but possesses a will to exist that is infinite. For finite existence cannot satisfy an infinite will; it is not what an infinite will desires.

4. There are three general modes of the human will to exist: two are necessarily infinite, the third is not. The first is the will to exist as an all-powerful, all-knowing, unlimited being which constitutes the universe or, indeed, all of reality. The second is to exist in and through another, that is, as a being encompassed by an infinite parent who provides peace, protection, and unending security. The third is the will to exist in and through one's own being even though that being is finite. These three modes of the will to exist are all present in the human person in infancy and childhood. In the course of time, as the person moves toward adulthood, one of these three modes of the will to exist becomes dominant. (This should be qualified: at times no one mode will dominate, resulting in conflict sufficiently intense to produce asoteria.) The mode of the will to exist that becomes dominant is a fundamental constituent of the personality and determines what the person generally and ultimately wants from life.

5. The reader will by now have recognized the first two modes of the will to exist enumerated above. The first, the desire to constitute all of reality and exist without bounds, forms the desire that is satisfied by the infinite personal response to the conflict of finitude. The second mode of the will to exist, to

exist infinitely in and through another, is satisfied by the infinite relational response. The third mode of the will to exist, to exist in and through one's own being although finite, has not yet been discussed. This mode will be referred to as *the substantive will.* The name substantive is derived from the term "substance," which has a rich philosophic history and possesses the basic meaning: "a being that subsists by and through itself; a separate and independent being."[8]

6. It is through the substantive will that a person who makes a finite response resolves the conflict of finitude and attains soteria. When the substantive mode of the will to exist becomes the dominant will, the infinite modes of the will to exist are for all practical purposes given up and play no further significant role in one's life. Thus the conflict of finitude is resolved. The substantive will's desire is to exist in and through one's own being, and it matters not that such being is finite. Accordingly, despite the psychic, physical, territorial, and existential boundaries that limit finite being, finite being satisfies the substantive will. The psyche that contains one's own authentic thoughts and feelings, the physical accomplishments of one's own body, the territory that consists of mutual relations with consenting persons and the just possession of things, and the existence that is deeply and genuinely experienced fulfill the dominant substantive mode of the will to exist and bring to those who make the finite response the ultimate meaningfulness of soteria.

Ontal Decisions

The process through which one of the three modes of the will to exist becomes dominant consists of a series of ontal decisions. Ontal decisions, which produce enduring changes in the fundamental structure of the human being, take place both consciously and unconsciously, and beginning with infancy require many years before they finally give lasting shape to the person's religion. When the necessary ontal decisions have been made, the person then exists in a state of soteria. When the ontal decisions required have not been made, the person will then exist in a state of dyssoteria or asoteria. In our time, the malaise of dyssoteria and the despair of asoteria are widespread.

Reasons for Accepting Response to the Conflict of Finitude as the Definition of Religion

The overall theme of this chapter has been that the definition of religion as "the human person's response to the conflict of finitude" should, at least in a polydox community, replace Western society's traditional definition of religion as "belief in theistic absolutism," that is, belief in an infinitely perfect personal deity who exercises supernatural care over humankind in this life, and provides infinite existence to the deserving in a hereafter. The reason is that "belief in theistic absolutism" as a definition of religion is neither sufficiently deep nor broad. It does not reveal the fundamental human activity of responding to finitude that religion expresses, nor does it include the full variety of ways in which finitude has been dealt with that have a semantic and logical right to be known and treated as religion. Without a definition of religion, of course, the freedom a polydox community affirms is blind. The community has freedom, but it has no notion of what it is to which the freedom pertains. With the definition of religion as "the human person's response to finitude," the freedom of the polydox community has focus and direction, and it affirms every member's right to respond to the conflict of finitude in a manner that brings the individual to soteria.

Semantic and logical analysis has shown that to define religion as "belief in theistic absolutism" is deficient. Compelling evidence of the definition's inadequacy also derives from Jewish "religious" history. The religious history of Jews is invaluable for an overview of religion in the Western world. For Jewish religious experience begins before the emergence of Pharisaic Judaism, whereas Christianity and Islam are both descendants of Pharisaism and dominated by its concepts. Consequently, Jews alone among the major Western religious communities possess non-Pharisaic religious origins, which produces a qualitative difference in the breadth and depth of their perspective on the uses of the word religion. This having been said, we may put the matter directly. The Jews over the ages have subscribed to systems of belief and practice that have been responses to the conflict of finitude, but which would not be "religion" defined as "belief in theistic absolutism." The following examples illustrate this point.

1. A cardinal principle of theistic absolutism is that there is an absolute separation between the being of the infinite, perfect deity and the finite and imperfect universe in general and the human person in particular. Yet pantheism, in which the deity, the universe, and the human person are united, is subscribed to explicitly by Kabbalist Jews and many early Hasidic Jews, and implicitly by the author of the Zohar and the Habad school of Hasidic Judaism. (Pantheism is commonly equated with atheism by theistic absolutists.)

2. Another cardinal principle of theistic absolutism is that the deity grants eternal life to the person; death is only the gateway to eternal life in a hereafter. Yet the prevailing belief of the Jewish "religious" systems preceding Pharisaism is that there is no afterlife and death is final. Thus belief in a hereafter appears nowhere as a belief of the religion of the Pentateuch or Torah. (There is no intention here to confuse the reader. It is true, as stated earlier, that the Pharisees employed the Pentateuch to provide evidence of a hereafter, but the interpretations of Scriptural passages they employed for this purpose have no basis in the text, and resemble more than anything else wishful thinking.) Moreover, the concept of a hereafter appears nowhere as a belief in any biblical system. Ecclesiastes explicitly rejects the notion.[9] Sadducean Judaism bitterly rejected the Pharisiac belief in an afterlife. Maimonides, in *The Guide of the Perplexed,* rejected belief in individual survival in an afterlife.[10]

3. Accordingly, the total theological experience of Jewish history requires an understanding of religion richer than "belief in theistic absolutism." To understand religion as "the human person's response to the conflict of finitude," however, makes clear that the different Jewish systems referred to above are clearly all religions, despite their essential differences.[11] The pantheistic Kabbalist and Hasidic systems are infinite personal response religions. Pharisaic Judaism is an infinite relational response religion. Pentateuchal (Torah) Judaism, and the Judaism of Ecclesiastes, the Sadducees, and Maimonides are finite response religions.

4. There is clearly no single religion called Judaism. Judaisms that prescribe diverse responses to finitude are simply different religions. All Judaisms, however, do share an essential purpose in common: this is to provide humans with responses to finitude that enable them to attain soteria. Hence the Judaisms of the ages can be referred to by a single term: the *Jewish religious complex*.[12] The function of the Jewish religious complex is not to serve the past but the living, to bring to humans of the present age whatever guidance they may require to reach soteria.

5. The definition of religion as "the human person's response to the conflict of finitude" enables us to apprehend sharply and clearly what is meant when a religion is said to be irrelevant or obsolete. A religion is irrelevant or obsolete when it fails to provide a response to finitude that brings soteria. The harsh judgment that history lays down on irrelevant religions is extinction.[13] Our analysis of the conflict of finitude reveals why this is so: the conflict of finitude produces in human persons the intolerable pain of meaningless existence. Humans must, therefore, in loyalty to that which is every person's primary responsibility, the authenticity and integrity of their own existences, seek out the religion and community that will provide them with soteria. The claim of a religious community to the loyalty of its members must ultimately rest on its ability to provide soteria. If it cannot provide this, experience teaches

us that all other claims to loyalty, on the basis of birth or nostalgia, for example, will prove empty.

Polydoxy and the Finite Response

The major categories of religion, or responses to the conflict of finitude, have been categorized as the infinite, discognitive, and finite responses. As has been stated, the infinite response has become increasingly ineffective in Western society. This has led to a striking increase in the numbers of persons who employ the discognitive response. The only alternative for persons who cannot subscribe to the infinite response, and who refuse to deal with the conflict of finitude in the unauthentic manner of a discognitive response, is to make a finite response. A finite response, however, requires knowledge, training, and an environment of support and approval. Only a polydoxy, which affirms its members' right and freedom to choose whichever response to finitude they wish, can institutionalize the finite response, and provide the instruction needed to understand the philosophy of the response, as well as the liturgy and rituals required to bring it concretely to the will and the emotions. The essence of a finite response is that persons can achieve and live in the meaningful state of soteria, even in the face of death's finality. Despite the fact that this finite response is often coupled with a belief in deity (even a supernatural deity, as in the Pentateuch and Prophets), orthodox theistic absolutistic religions look upon the soterial claim of the finite response as hubristic and sinfully presumptuous. They insist that without the gracious and miraculous gift of infinite existence there can be no soteria. Only in the polydox community, which teaches and approves of all responses to the conflict of finitude, can the finite response be institutionalized, and the environment of affirmation, approval, and insight that is necessary for the finite response to bring soteria be created.

Notes

1. A traditionoid religion is to be distinguished from a traditional

religion. A traditional religion (see p. 86) is one handed down from the past; a traditionoid religion *appears* to have been handed down from the past but is, in fact, one invented by its adherents.

2. I divide all views on the word God into four major categories: *theopanism, theosupernaturalism, theonaturalism,* and *atheonomatism.* In theopanism the meaning given the word God is of an entity that is not separate from the universe. Theopanism includes pantheism and panentheism. In theosupernaturalism the meaning given the word God is of an entity or entities who are separate from the universe, and who have the power to interrupt the natural course of the universe. Theosupernaturalism includes theistic absolutism. In theonaturalism the meaning given the word God is of an entity that is separate from the universe, and that creates the natural universe or is the ground of the natural universe. There are no miraculous interruptions of the processes of the universe in theonaturalism; natural laws and forces entirely govern human and all other existence. Theonaturalism includes deism and hylotheism. Atheonomatism is the view that the word God has no reality meaning, that is, the word God refers to no real being of any kind. Atheonomatism includes atheism (as the term is commonly used) and agnosticism. See *Polydoxy,* Vol. 4, No. 1, 1979.

3. I have taken *soteria* from the Greek word for salvation, but I employ it neutrally, without any necessary nuance of supernaturalism which is often attached to the term salvation.

4. As has been noted, Pharisaic Judaism exists today unchanged except for minor details as Orthodox Judaism.

5. Cf. pp. 109 ff.

6. For reasons similar to those given for the rejection of Orthodox Judaism, see pp. 100 ff. and 123 ff.

7. There are several reasons for this, perhaps the most important of which is that an awareness of finity and reality emerges in consciousness during adolescence that is qualitatively more heightened than that which is present in childhood. This produces a sudden and highly intensified conflict of finitude in persons who are relatively young and inexperienced in coping with existence.

8. *The Encyclopedia of Philosophy* (N.Y., 1972 ed.), *s.v.* "substance" (particularly Spinoza's use).

9. Ecclesiastes 3:19 f.

10. Part I, Chap. 74.

11. The criterion by which different religions are distinguished from one another is discussed in detail in the following chapter, pp. 95 ff.

12. This same thought can arguably be applied to the totality of religious systems referred to by the term *Christianity.* Replacing *Christianity* by *Christian religious complex* makes it clear that the various Christian religions are, in fact, *different* religions; see p. 185.

13. See pp. 197 ff.

Chapter IV

The Ratio-Moral Authority Principle

Misconceptions Regarding the
Present Religious Situation of Jews

Owing to the significant role that the religious beliefs of Jews have played in the history of Western Civilization, particularly as regards Christianity, an understanding of the present religious situation among Jews is of more than Jewish interest. The purpose of the ensuing analysis is to provide this understanding. The task, however, is a complicated one, for there are three basic misconceptions regarding the contemporary religious life of Jews, widely held by Jews and non-Jews alike,[1] which make understanding the contemporary Jewish religious situation difficult:

1. The notion that contemporary Jews have one religion, not several religions.[2]
2. The notion that this one contemporary Jewish religion is either Orthodox Judaism or one of several variations that is essentially similar to Orthodox Judaism.[3] Orthodox Judaism and its ostensible essential variations will be treated as one religion and referred to as the *Orthodox Jewish Cognate Complex.*
3. The notion that the most general fundamental principle underlying the contemporary religious life of Jews is belief in a supernatural covenant between Jews and a theistic deity.

Reasons for the Misconceptions

Why are these misconceptions so widely accepted? The fact that
these reasons are more psychological and sociological than substantive and theological suggests that unmaking these notions
will more often be met with an emotional rather than intellectual
response.

1. Each institution representing one of the religions of the Jews
   endoctrines its members with the idea that there is only one
   Jewish religion. Perhaps the chief means of accomplishing
   this endoctrining is the semantic device whereby each institution refers to itself as "Judaism," omitting the essential qualifying adjective, "Orthodox," "Reform," or the like.[4]

2. The idea that there is more than one religion among the Jews
   is deeply disturbing to those Jews who wish to view all Jews
   as constituting a single collective entity. A variety of reasons,
   political,[5] institutional, economic, as well as psychological, lie
   behind this wish. It is unnecessary for our purpose here to
   examine all these reasons, but one illustration will be useful.
   If it is the case that among the Jews there exist different
   religions, so that Orthodox Judaism is a different religion
   from Reform Judaism, then Reform Jews whose parents or
   grandparents are Orthodox subscribe to a different religion
   from that of some of their closest family relations. Recognition of such a state of affairs could produce feelings of guilt,
   disloyalty, or other painful emotions in many Reform Jews.
   Accordingly, it is vastly preferable for these persons to maintain the belief that Orthodox Judaism and Reform Judaism
   are essentially the same religion with only insignificant differences between them.

3. The idea that there are different Jewish religions in the present
   cannot help but lead to the consideration that religions such
   as Orthodox Judaism and Reform Judaism are not only different religions from each other but different religions from
   those of Jews in the past which appear in the Bible and other
   historical religious works. The discovery that their religion is

not the same as that of their ostensible forebears would cause many Jews great concern. The view, then, that there is only one present-day Judaism contributes to avoidance of this disagreeable discovery.

4. Many Christians believe and wish to continue believing that Jews have one religion, and that this religion is the Orthodox Jewish Cognate Complex. There are numerous and diverse reasons for this being so, but the following are the most important and suffice for this discussion.

   A. The thinking of Christians regarding the religious life of Jews derives generally from the New Testament where Jewish religion primarily means Pharisaic Judaism,[6] which is essentially the same as Orthodox Judaism. These Christians expect, therefore, the religious life of Jews to be as the New Testament describes it.

   B. The truth of the New Testament is recognized by New Testament Christians[7] as dependent upon the Bible (Old Testament) being fundamentally true.[8] If the Bible's claim of being supernatural revelation from a theistic God is false, then the Bible's fundamental teaching is false, the New Testament is false, and New Testament Christianity is false. Thus, at the very least, it would be psychologically damaging to the credibility of New Testament Christianity if Jews themselves, among whose forebears the Bible arose, and whose ancestral religions regarded it as supernatural revelation, should now after critical examination decide the Bible is of questionable veracity or simply false. It is understandable, consequently, that New Testament Christians should want "Judaism" to affirm the Bible as true inasmuch as this would provide their beliefs with the color of corroboration. The contemporary Judaism that affirms the fundamental truth of the Bible is Orthodox Judaism. Accordingly, it is of considerable benefit to New Testament Christians to believe that Jews have only one religion, and that that religion is the Orthodox Jewish Cognate Complex.

C. Believing they possess the ultimate truth and key to salvation, New Testament Christians, understandably, do not wish to see the emergence of a non-New Testament Christianity, such as Polydox Christianity, that would present Christians with an alternative to the New Testament Christianities. Orthodox Judaism possesses fundamental beliefs sufficiently similar to those of New Testament Christianity to encourage the thought among Christians that if Jews can have different religions, including polydox religion, so too can Christians. Thus by maintaining the notion that Jews have but one religion, the Orthodox Jewish Cognate Complex, New Testament Christians can prevent knowledge of non-Orthodox religions among the Jews from reaching Christians and encouraging them to develop non-New Testament Christian religions.

5. The fact that Christians largely believe that the Orthodox Jewish Cognate Complex is the religion of contemporary Jews has influenced some Jews, who in order not to disappoint Christian expectations, profess the Orthodox Jewish Cognate Complex as their religion despite the fact that they may neither practice, believe, nor even understand its teachings. Jews are particularly tempted to do this since many New Testament Christians express a special feeling of relationship with Orthodox Jews, owing to the former's belief that Orthodox Judaism not only is a precursor of Christianity, but shares in principle its fundamental beliefs as well. One can easily sympathize with the desire of Jews, who generally comprise minorities in countries with Christian majorities, to conform to Christian expectations.[9] Still, such conformity prevents Jews from understanding the basic nature of contemporary Jewish religious life, and from acquiring authentic insight into themselves.

6. There are Jews and non-Jews alike who take the position that there is no religion of Jews that is relevant to or competent for the modern age. These persons have no difficulty in rejecting Orthodox Judaism on critical[10] and moral grounds.[11]

Accordingly, if the Orthodox Jewish Cognate Complex were the only religion among Jews, the position that there is no Jewish religion relevant to the modern world could be established by its advocates to their satisfaction without difficulty. Thus we may expect these advocates to resist the view that there is more than one religion among the Jews, especially that there is a polydox religion, which is not subject to the critical and moral objections to which Orthodox Judaism is vulnerable.

Faith

Before proceeding further, it is necessary to turn our attention to the term *faith*. As is well known, the term has had a lengthy history and numerous different meanings. We will use the term faith in its philosophic sense to refer to "the mental act of assent that judges a tenet, statement, or proposition to be true."[12] The word *belief* will be employed as a synonym of the term *faith*. Thus if the proposition is asserted "a theistic God exists,"[13] the act of faith or believing is assent to the truth of this proposition, the judgment that the proposition is true.[14]

Evidential and Nonevidential Faith

A proposition can be faithed either on the basis of evidence or without evidence. Persons differ regarding the requirement of evidence for faithing propositions. There are those who require evidence for all propositions that are to be given faith; other persons require evidence for faithing certain propositions, such as those of science, but not for faithing other propositions, those of religion, for example. Accordingly, faith can be divided into two general categories, evidential and nonevidential. *Evidential faith* requires evidence for assent to the truth of a belief or proposition; *nonevidential faith* requires no evidence for assent to a belief's or proposition's truth. Among those who employ evidence for faith, the kind of evidence required differs. Three broad classes of evidence can be distinguished: *objective, subjective,* and *dixit.*

Objective Evidence

Objective evidence is defined as evidence that possesses two characteristics: first, it is apprehended publicly, by more than one person; second, it is apprehended by ordinary human faculties functioning naturally, that is, through sensation operating together with reason,[15] or through reason alone.[16]

Objective evidence is divided into two kinds, *unrepeatable* and *repeatable.* Unrepeatable objective evidence is that which is apprehended publicly and naturally, but which cannot be apprehended by human effort at will so that it can be experienced whenever desired. The evidence for the revelation at Mount Sinai, as recounted in the Pentateuch, provides an instance of unrepeatable objective evidence. According to the Bible, the evidence consisted of the Israelites publicly apprehending through natural sensing and reasoning an event that will never occur again.[17] Since the event never recurs, objective evidence of the event, which necessarily involves sensing it, cannot recur, and the evidence of the event is therefore unrepeatable. Events need not be ranked as miracles to be regarded as unrepeatable. All past events that are taken as essentially unique,[18] natural or miraculous, are events for which the objective evidence is unrepeatable.

Repeatable objective evidence is that which is apprehended publicly and naturally, and which can be experienced at will by humans to prove whatever belief or proposition it may be for which it serves as evidence. Consequently, all observers who wish to can witness repeatable objective evidence.[19] Repeatable objective evidence is the evidence not only of the physical sciences today, but of ancient and medieval metaphysical or theological science. Cosmological, teleological, and ontological proofs of the existence of a being that was called God can be experienced repeatedly. Any number of persons, by understanding the premises and deducing the consequences, can test these proofs any number of times.[20]

Subjective Evidence

Subjective evidence is defined as evidence that is apprehended privately by one person alone. Like objective evidence, subjective evidence is divided into two kinds, unrepeatable and repeatable. Unlike objective evidence, subjective evidence can be apprehended supernaturally as well as naturally.[21]

Natural subjective evidence includes natural sensations experienced by a person when alone and at no time by anyone else, natural reasoning by a person that is neither communicable nor comprehensible to anyone else, and introspections of imaginations, dreams, desires, and feelings all of which by their nature are experienced privately.[22] Supernatural subjective evidence is that which is apprehended in a miraculous manner. The vision of Abraham reported in Genesis 15 is an illustration of supernatural subjective evidence.[23] Abraham, according to the story, received a communication or prophecy miraculously from the deity Yahveh when in a deep sleep, an event that occurred privately within the confines of his psyche. Mystical experiences likewise provide supernatural subjective evidence. Probably the most common experience that provides supernatural subjective evidence is the "feeling" of relationship with a "presence" that many persons say they experience when praying to a theistic deity.[24]

Unrepeatable subjective evidence is that which is apprehended by a person privately, and which cannot be repeated at will by the person's effort or that of any other human. Supernatural subjective evidence such as the prophetic dreams and visions the Bible reports Abraham and other prophets experienced would constitute unrepeatable subjective evidence inasmuch as they were allegedly miracles that came from Yahveh and could not be reproduced at will by human effort. Mystical experiences are generally reported by mystics as overtaking them independent of their will. Repeatable subjective evidence includes sensations and self-data that can be privately experienced by a person whenever desired. The supernatural communication with a theistic god or other divine presences that some persons report takes place in prayer, for example, is claimed by many of them to be attainable whenever they wish.

Dixit Evidence

Dixit evidence consists solely of statements or assertions that some human person has made.[25] In other words, when persons assent or give faith to a belief on the basis of dixit evidence, they have no evidence for the truth of the belief other than that which they have been told by some human individual or group. Note that what is objective or subjective evidence for those who experience such evidence directly becomes dixit evidence for those who are told about the evidence but have not themselves experienced it directly.

The form of dixit evidence formally employed by religions historically is termed "tradition." Tradition, as defined generally in religious philosophy, consists of beliefs that are handed down from members of one generation to those of a succeeding generation with the assurance of the former to the latter that the beliefs are true. Tradition is dixit evidence, of course, because all that the members of the succeeding generation have to justify giving faith to what they believe is the bare word of members of the previous generation which tells them what the beliefs are and that the beliefs are true. Tradition is of critical importance to a present-day community whose religion ultimately is based entirely upon an ancient Scripture, for the community has only traditional, that is, dixit evidence to testify to the truth of its Scripture.[26] If dixit evidence should be considered invalid,[27] the Scripture would be without evidence of its truth, and the religion could not justify faith.

Nonevidential Faith

Nonevidential faith is assent to the truth of a proposition or belief without evidence of any kind. Often there are reasons why persons give nonevidential faith to a belief, but it must be noted that these reasons have nothing to do with establishing the truth of the belief. Prominent among these reaons are: loyalty to parents or to a native religious community, blind trust, a will to believe, a desire for the feelings of security and comfort that the belief may give, ignorance of critical thinking, guilt, or fear that blocks the ability to think critically. Whatever the reason for giving nonevidential faith may be, it is not evidence that establishes the truth of the belief. Among other names given at times to nonevidential faith are *blind faith* and *leap of faith*. The leap involved is jumping from awareness of a belief to giving faith to it without possessing evidence to justify assent to its truth.

Cognitive and Noncognitive Faith

The term faith has been defined as the "act of assent that judges a tenet, statement, or proposition to be true." Used in this sense, faith is a cognitive act in that it is part of the cognitive or "knowing" process. The term *cognitive faith* can be applied to this kind of faith. There are also noncognitive kinds of faith, namely, faith that describes actions that are not part of the knowing process. Such faith will be referred to as *noncognitive faith*. The most prevalent form of noncognitive faith described by theologians and religionists is faith as an act of trust in and dependence upon a deity who (or that) is not conceptualized.[28] Accordingly, in noncognitive faith, no cognitive acts are performed, such as formulating a concept of God or other beliefs, examining the evidence that exists for the truth of the concept or belief, and assenting to the truth of the concept or belief. Persons who give noncognitive faith, like those who give faith without evidence, are also characterized as giving blind faith or engaging in a leap of faith. The reason for the characterization of blind faith is that without conceptualization the giver of faith has no idea of whom or what the object of trust and dependence is, or even whether the object exists. Such faith is a leap of faith because it "leaps over" or bypasses the cognitive process.

Forms of Cognitive Faith

Returning to the subject of cognitive faith, six forms can be described. Ranked according to how convincing they are generally considered to be, these forms are: *faith on the basis of repeatable objective evidence;*[29] *faith on the basis of unrepeatable objective evidence; faith on the basis of repeatable subjective evidence; faith on the basis of unrepeatable subjective evidence; faith on the basis of dixit evidence;* and *faith without evidence.*

1. *Repeatable objective evidence* is generally considered to be the most compelling evidence for faith. The reason for this lies in four characteristics repeatable objective evidence possesses. First, it is apprehended either through the five senses in combination with reason or through reason alone,—and for most persons the apprehensions of the senses and reason are valid evidence of truth.[30] Second, repeatable objective evidence is apprehended publicly, by more than one person. This greatly reduces the possibility of error, illusion, or hallucination that exists when only one person can witness evidence and no one else can corroborate it. Third, repeatable objective evidence can be experienced at will, and therefore, can be verified by all interested persons whenever they wish. Thus there is no need for anyone to rely for the evidence upon the hearsay of tradition or other dixit evidence. Fourth, since repeatable objective evidence can be experienced at will, even persons who already have witnessed the evidence can, if doubts should arise about the accuracy of their memories, reexperience the evidence for reexamination.
2. *Unrepeatable objective evidence* is generally regarded as less

credible than repeatable objective evidence. Although unrepeatable objective evidence does possess two of the characteristics of repeatable objective evidence—apprehension through the senses and reason or through reason alone—unrepeatable objective evidence lacks the other two features that give repeatable objective evidence its compelling force—the capacity to be experienced and reexamined at will. The result is that unrepeatable objective evidence requires everyone other than the persons who apprehended it directly to accept the evidence as valid on the basis of the latter's bare say-so, that is, as dixit evidence. Moreover, seeing that the evidence is unrepeatable, should those who experienced it directly become subject to doubts regarding the accuracy of their memories, there would be no way to reexamine and reevaluate their original experiences. Furthermore, if conflicts should arise among the memories of the persons who experienced the evidence, there would be no way for those who received from these persons their information regarding the evidence to determine which conflicting report is true.

3. *Repeatable subjective evidence* encounters even more highly significant problems of credibility than does unrepeatable objective evidence. Repeatable subjective evidence is experienced by only one person so that, unlike objective evidence, there is no other person able to verify that it ever existed. The person who experiences repeatable subjective evidence, however, owing to the fact that it can be reproduced as desired, is able to reexperience and reexamine it to satisfy whatever personal doubts may arise regarding its accuracy. Since repeatable subjective evidence is apprehended by only one person, it can only have the status of dixit evidence for everyone other than the person who experiences it.

4. *Unrepeatable subjective evidence,* like repeatable subjective evidence, presents the problem of necessarily being dixit evidence for everyone other than the person who experiences it, but, in addition, presents a serious problem even for the one who does experience it. For if doubts should arise in the

mind of the latter regarding the accuracy of her or his memory of the evidence or whether the evidence ever indeed existed, there would be no way in which to reexperience the evidence for reexamination. Moreover, unlike unrepeatable objective evidence, where the memories of other persons who allegedly witnessed the same event can be called upon for corroboration, the person who uses unrepeatable subjective evidence has only a private past experience upon which to rely.[31]

5. *Dixit evidence* poses even more significant problems than the preceding forms of evidence for those who rely upon it to justify their faith. We may take it that all human beings are fallible, subject in varying degrees to sensory illusions, misconceptions, delusions, and hallucinations. Yet those who employ dixit evidence must use the unsupported statement of just such fallible beings as the sole basis of their faith. Moreover, there is the problem of conflicting dixit evidence. It often happens that one person will assert a belief to be true that contradicts the belief that another person asserts to be true. How, in such a case, is a person who accepts dixit evidence to determine which belief is true since both assertions equally have the support of dixit evidence? Religions that employ dixit evidence, or as it is usually termed in such use, *tradition,* on which to base all or some of their beliefs, attempt to deal with this problem by claiming that those who hand down the dixit evidence from one generation to the next have been exceptionally trustworthy.[32] Still, when a neutral and unbiased observer looks at those who are said to have transmitted the traditions of Orthodox Judaism, Roman Catholic Christianity, and Sunni Islam, it is difficult to see how the persons who have transmitted the tradition of one of these religions can be said to be more trustworthy than those who have handed down the traditions of the other two, yet each tradition dogmatically asserts the truth of beliefs that are not only different but contradictory. It is important to emphasize that the fundamental beliefs of such religions as Orthodox

Judaism, Roman Catholicism, and Sunni Islam must be accepted by their adherents today entirely on the basis of dixit evidence.[33] For the validity of the basic tenets of these religions rests solely on the truth of their respective ancient Scriptures, and the only evidence now available for the truth of these Scriptures is the dixit evidence of each religion's particular tradition. That is to say, all that exists today as evidence that an ancient Scripture, such as the Bible, New Testament, or Koran, is true is testimony that allegedly has been transmitted to the present from one generation to the next beginning with the generation that supposedly witnessed firsthand the events recorded in the Scripture. No method has been provided by those who accept the dixit evidence of one of the above religions that enables a neutral and unbiased observer to determine that their religion's tradition is trustworthy and that those of the other two religions are not.

6. *Faith without evidence,* assent to the truth of a proposition or belief for which the believer has no evidence of any kind, gives rise to numerous difficulties. For one, it leaves the believer entirely without criteria by which to judge the validity of the belief. Consequently, inasmuch as faith without evidence is wholly blind, believers have no way to distinguish among different beliefs all of which equally lack evidence. Thus faith without evidence believers cannot distinguish between the fantasies created by finite human need and beliefs that are rooted in reality. Yet faith without evidence, even though it is assent that is entirely without justification, violates no rule of logic and is given by many adherents to the beliefs of their religions.

Evidence for Faith among Jewish Religious Systems

In every Jewish[34] religious system prior to the nineteenth century, the essential reason for the faith has been objective evidence, either unrepeatable objective evidence alone, repeatable objective evidence, or unrepeatable objective evidence in combination with dixit evidence, that is, tradition. In other words, no pre-nine-teenth century Jewish religious system claimed to be true or asked to be believed without presenting objective evidence, alone or in combination. Subjective evidence was never employed; and certainly, no pre-nineteenth century Jewish system requested faith of its adherents because it satisfied a need or will to believe.

The illustration par excellence of a pre-nineteenth century Jewish religious system that was based on unrepeatable objective evidence is the religion of the generation of Jews who, according to the pentateuchal account, lived at the time of Moses.[35] According to the Pentateuch, these Jews witnessed firsthand the Sinaitic revelation and other miraculous events that took place during their journey with Moses through the wilderness and served as evidence of the truth of the pentateuchal religion.[36] Such evidence was objective in that it was both witnessed publicly by many persons,[37] and apprehended naturally, through the ordinary human powers of sensing and understanding. On the other hand, this evidence was unrepeatable because, according to the Pentateuch, the Sinaitic revelation and other miracles performed through Moses would never again occur.[38]

The pre-nineteenth century Jewish religious systems that were based upon repeatable objective evidence consisted primarily of the medieval philosophic religions, among which Maimonides' system is the prime example. Maimonides held that a person could give genuine faith to a belief only on the basis of empirical and rational evidence so convincing that it compelled the intellect to assent to the belief's truth.[39] Such evidence had to be experienced by the believer directly and could not, therefore, be communicated by tradition.[40] So, for example, Maimonides' fundamental proof for the existence of a deity was the cosmological argument, a proof based upon natural empirical and rational processes common to all members of the human species, and which provides direct evidence for the belief it justifies. Consequently, the cosmological argument can be tested at will by every person who studies and understands it.[41]

The most widespread of the pre-nineteenth century Jewish

religions were those based on unrepeatable objective evidence in combination with the dixit evidence of tradition. The reason is that the foundation of these religions was the Bible, primarily the Pentateuch. Since the statements and claims of the Pentateuch, by the Pentateuch's own account, could be verified directly only by the generation of Jews who lived at the time of Moses, the sole means by which the Pentateuch could be verified as true by the generations who came after Moses was through the dixit evidence of tradition.

The two major Jewish religions based on unrepeatable objective evidence in combination with the dixit evidence of tradition are Sadduceeism and Pharisaism. It is significant to note that the fundamental difference between these two religious systems lies in the way their traditions regard the revelation Moses is described in the Pentateuch as receiving from the deity Yahveh at Mount Sinai and on subsequent occasions. The Sadducees, on the basis of their dixit evidence, claimed Moses received only the Pentateuch; the Pharisees, based on their dixit evidence, claimed Moses received the Pentateuch and the Talmud. Since the beliefs of the Talmud radically altered the nature of pentateuchal religion, essential differences existed between Sadducean and Pharisaic religion.[42] Sadduceeism came to an effective end with the destruction of the Temple in Jerusalem in 70 C.E.[43] Pharisaic Judaism, consequently, became the dominant religion among the Jews in late antiquity, continued its dominance in the Middle Ages, in which period we commonly refer to it as Rabbinic Judaism, and survives in the modern age by the name Orthodox Judaism.

Orthodox Judaism

Entering into the nineteenth century, Orthodox Judaism was still the dominant Jewish religion and adhered to by almost all Jews. Accordingly, it is with Orthodox Judaism that our analysis of contemporary Judaism begins. The central dogma of Orthodox Judaism is that the story of the Sinaitic revelation recorded in the Pentateuch is literally and infallibly true, as is every word written in the Pentateuch. This story, in brief, is that Moses and the Jews at Mount Sinai received a revelation which climaxed a series of previous revelations to Abraham and his Jewish descendents.[44] In this revelation, Yahveh, the theistic God who created the universe, entered into a covenant with the Jews and communicated to them his will, namely, the commandments he enjoined them to obey. These commandments are contained in the Pentateuch and the Talmud along with other commandments revealed to Moses on the journey through the wilderness subsequent to the Sinaitic revelation.

From this central dogma, Orthodox Judaism derives the following essential beliefs:

1. There is only one god, Yahveh, who is an omniscient, omnipotent, omnibenevolent, and eternal person.
2. Yahveh is the sole creator and conserver of the universe.
3. Yahveh in his omniscience is aware of humans, and in his omnipotence and omnibenevolence exercises supernatural providence over human affairs.
4. Yahveh communicated the Pentateuch and Talmud to Moses through a verbal revelation,[45] and they are, therefore, literally and infallibly true.
5. There has never been, nor will there ever be, a revelation from the creator God of the universe that supersedes the revelation to Moses contained in the Pentateuch and the Talmud.
6. Inasmuch as Orthodox Judaism consists of the doctrines of the Pentateuch and the Talmud, Orthodox Judaism is the only true religion there is or ever will be. There has never been and will never be another Judaism, and no other religion is true.
7. Every commandment in the Pentateuch and Talmud must be obeyed by the Jews to whom they are directed.[46] There is no way in which a person born a Jew can ever become free of her or his obligation to obey the commandments of the Pentateuch and Talmud. Even if a Jew converts to another

religion, or otherwise renounces the Sinaitic covenant and Orthodox Judaism, the obligation to obey the commandments remains, and those who fail to do so are accounted sinners.

8. All persons are endowed with freedom of the will. Thus Yahveh rewards those who observe his commandments and punishes those who do not. Yahveh's administering of divine retribution provides the fundamental dynamic of history; the great movements and events of history result from Yahveh rewarding and punishing individuals and nations.[47]

9. The Jews are Yahveh's chosen people, and the recipients, therefore, of his special providence and favor.

10. There is a supernatural end to human history, the Messianic Age, which will be ushered in by a Messiah. In the Messianic Age, humans will be resurrected and judged by Yahveh, receiving rewards for their good deeds and punishment for their sins.

11. There is a human afterlife of individual consciousness and sublime corporeality.

Criterion for Distinguishing Different Religions

At this point in the discussion, a question must be raised. How do we determine whether two or more religions constitute the same religion or different ones? This question is a novel one. Like many basic questions in the history of thought, the question of the criterion whereby religions are judged to be the same or distinct from one another has generally gone unrecognized, and consequently, unanswered. This necessitates that it be dealt with explicitly here. Accordingly, the steps in the reasoning underlying the choice of the criterion to be used will first be enumerated, and then the criterion itself stated.

1. Religions have fundamentally psychic or mental existence, that is, they exist primarily in the human psyche or mind, and only derivatively or secondarily in the sensible world. Religions are often confused, of course, with concrete sense

objects such as ritual actions and objects, service books, buildings, and physical symbols of various kinds. These concrete sense objects in themselves, however, have no meaning or value without the beliefs and other psychic contents that religionists direct toward them.

2. The psychic contents that constitute religions are the beliefs,[48] desires, and emotions that pertain to the religion. Illustrating this from a theistic religion:[49] a belief is the affirmation that some particular theistic deity exists; a desire is reflected by wanting to obey the commandments of the theistic deity; and emotion is expressed by loving the theistic deity.

3. Of the three kinds of psychic contents that make up religions, beliefs are the basic constituents. Without beliefs, desires and emotions are blind; they have neither object nor purpose. Thus if Orthodox Judaism did not set forth the belief that Yahveh is God; Roman Catholicism, that the Trinity is the Godhead; and Sunni Islam, that Allah is God; Orthodox Jews, Roman Catholics, and Sunnites could not have a desire to obey the commandments of their respective deities, or feel emotions of love toward them.

4. The beliefs of a religion are divided into essential and nonessential categories. Beliefs in the essential category are those that the religion states must be believed by every adherent; nonessential beliefs are those the religion declares optional. Essential and nonessential beliefs may relate to ideology, ritual observance, or morality.

5. The essential beliefs of a religion constitute the religion; they make a religion the religion it is. Or, in other words, the essential beliefs of a religion constitute its definition. Thus a person who accepts the essential beliefs of a religion is an adherent of the religion; a person who rejects any essential belief of a religion rejects the religion. (The reason is that a religion is nothing other than its essential beliefs so that a person who rejects any of these beliefs simply does not believe in the religion it is.)

6. Essential beliefs cannot be reduced to general concepts by a

process of abstraction. To illustrate: Orthodox Judaism sets forth among its essential beliefs that there is a theistic God named Yahveh, who is the creator God of the universe and who requires obedience to the Bible and the Talmud, the only true revelation in the present age; Roman Catholicism teaches as essential beliefs that there is a theistic trinitarian Godhead, consisting of a Father, Son, and Holy Spirit, unified in one substance, who is the creator God of the universe, who requires obedience, and whose ultimate revelation was made in the Incarnation of Jesus Christ; Sunni Islam asserts as essential beliefs that there is a theistic god called Allah, who is the creator God of the universe and who requires obedience to the Koran, the only true revelation in the present age. Since each of these religious systems asserts the existence of some kind of theism as an essential belief, the temptation exists to abstract from each one's particular theistic concept the generalization that all subscribe to basically the same concept of God, theism. This generalization would be erroneous. The essential belief of Orthodox Judaism is that Yahveh is God, of Roman Catholicism, that the Trinity is the Godhead, and of Sunnism, that Allah is God. None of these religions holds that theism in general is true; each, on the contrary, insists only its particular concept of theism is true and that the other theisms are false. To concretize this point: if a member of the Orthodox Jewish community, the Roman Catholic community, or the Sunnite community were to say that she or he did not believe in the particular theism of her or his community, but rather in a general or universal theism in which the deity revealed himself equally to every human heart, she or he would be declared a heretic by the community. For to Orthodox Judaism, Roman Catholicism, and Sunni Islam, a general theism is as false as each one's particular theism is to the others.

7. Since its essential beliefs make a religion the religion it is, religions that have identical essential beliefs constitute the same religion.[50] Also, religions that have identical essential

beliefs but different nonessential beliefs constitute the same religion.[51] Accordingly, *the criterion for determining that religions are the same is that their essential beliefs are identical.*

8. Since its essential beliefs make a religion the religion it is, religions that do not possess identical essential beliefs are different religions.[52] Accordingly, *the criterion for determining that religions are different from one another is that their essential beliefs are nonidentical.*

9. We arrive, then, at the final point, the criterion for determining that one essential belief is nonidentical with another. This criterion may be formulated thusly: Essential beliefs are nonidentical with one another if they cannot at the same time be affirmed as true by a single mind without the mind falling into self-contradiction. In other words, nonidentical essential beliefs cannot be assented to simultaneously by a coherent, unified mind, for they are logically mutually exclusive. This point is easily illustrated by comparing the following three propositions, the first made up of essential beliefs from Orthodox Judaism, the second of essential beliefs from Roman Catholicism, and the third from Sunni Islam.

A. Yahveh is the creator God of the universe, and his true revelation, which must be believed and obeyed now and for all human history,[53] is the Bible.

B. The trinitarian Godhead of Father, Son, and Holy Spirit is the creator God of the universe, and the Godhead's last and definitive act of revelation, which must be believed now and for all human history, is the Incarnation of Jesus Christ as interpreted by the Roman Catholic Church.

C. Allah is the creator God of the universe, and his true revelation, which must be believed and obeyed now and for all human history, is the Koran.

Clearly enough, these three sets of essential beliefs cannot be believed by a single mind at the same time without its falling into self-contradiction. Accordingly, the three religions, each of which professes a different one of these sets of beliefs, constitutes three different religions.

The Creation of New Jewish Religions

Orthodox Judaism, as stated earlier, can be regarded as having been the religion of practically all Jews at the beginning of the nineteenth century. New conditions emerged, however, before the century was over, that produced a massive onslaught upon the faith of Jews in the essential beliefs of Orthodoxy. These essential beliefs of Orthodoxy are summarized in the list enumerated below.[54] Note that the first essential belief, "there exists a true and infallible revelation, the Mosaic revelation," is the foundation of the rest. For all the other essential beliefs are derived from the Mosaic revelation, and, in addition, the only evidence of their truth is its truth. Accordingly, if the Mosaic revelation is false, the other essential beliefs are themselves either false or unsupported assertions without evidence of truth.

1. There exists a true and infallible revelation, the Mosaic revelation, consisting of the Pentateuch and the Talmud.
2. There is only one God of the universe, the being referred to and described in the Pentateuch and Talmud as Yahveh. Yahveh is an eternal person, omnipotent, omniscient, and omnibenevolent.
3. Yahveh, the perfect being, communicated the Pentateuch and Talmud to Moses by verbal revelation, and they are, therefore, literally and infallibly true.
4. Yahveh is the sole creator and conserver of the universe.
5. Yahveh in his omniscience is aware of humans, and in his omnipotence and omnibenevolence exercises supernatural providence over human affairs.
6. The revelation of the Pentateuch and Talmud to Moses perfectly expresses the will of Yahveh, namely, that which Yahveh wants humankind to believe and do. No other revelation has occurred or will occur in human history that has altered or will alter this statement of God's will or the obligation of humans to obey its commandments.

7. Inasmuch as Orthodox Judaism consists of the one and only revelation from the deity, it is the only true religion.
8. There is an ideal and supernatural end to human history, the Messianic Era, which will be ushered in by a Messiah.
9. There is an afterlife consisting of resurrection and eternal life.
10. Yahveh rewards those who observe his commandments and punishes those who do not. There is retribution in this life, in the Messianic Era, and in the afterlife.

Conditions Challenging Belief in Orthodox Judaism

These new conditions, brought about before the nineteenth century was over, challenged belief in Orthodoxy indirectly and directly. Indirectly, they created an environment inhospitable to and incongruent with the truth of Orthodoxy's essential beliefs and the validity of its rituals. Directly, they denied and rejected the truth of Orthodoxy's essential beliefs. These new conditions, although organically interrelated and mutually reinforcing, can be divided for analysis into five categories: political, economic, social, cultural, and intellectual. In discussing these new conditions, the intent is not to describe them in detail, a task for historians, but to identify them and point out the influence they wielded upon the religious beliefs of Jews.[55]

Political conditions: Two prime points bear mentioning here.

1. History teaches that, except for rare spirits, persons do not take positions regarding religious beliefs for which they will be punished or otherwise harassed by the government of the country in whch they live. Consciously or unconsciously, they conceal opinions they view as politically dangerous.[56] It is only when they can speak their minds with impunity that most people can allow themselves to arrive at and act on their true religious beliefs. Freedom from government regulation or reprisal respecting religious thought and expression will be referred to as *political religious freedom.*[57] The denial of polit-

ical religious freedom has generally taken place in countries where there is an official religion.[58] An official religion is one that is supported by the state, either as the religion of a theocratic state, or as an established religion, namely, a religion recognized by law as the official religion of the state and supported by civil authority.[59] Such governments have usually insisted that their subjects or citizens all profess the official religion, or at the least, that no one express views that might subvert or weaken the credibility of the official religion. In antiquity and through the Middle Ages to the beginning of the nineteenth century, Jews in the main did not possess political religious freedom.[60] Moreover, from the Middle Ages on, they almost all lived in countries where either a Christian or Muslim religion was the official religion, and where, as followers primarily of Orthodox Judaism, they lacked political religious freedom and were viewed as infidels.[61] As such, they were periodically either exiled or tolerated. One should bear in mind that the perception by Christians and Muslims that the religion of Jews was Orthodox Judaism was an important factor in helping to justify and bring about these periods of toleration. For Orthodox Judaism could be understood as supporting Christian and Muslim religions. By asserting the truth of the Bible, Orthodox Judaism corroborated an essential belief of Christian and Muslim religions, although they maintained their revelations and religions transcended it. Moreover, by declaring the truth of the pentateuchal Mosaic revelation, Orthodoxy testified in principle to the notions that theism is true and supernatural events occur, both basic features of Christian and Muslim religions. Since Orthodoxy, therefore, had value for countries where Christian and Muslim religions were the official religions and Jews were only tolerated, it would have been perilous for any Jew to repudiate Orthodoxy and replace it with a religion that, for example, denied the Bible was revelation or in any other way attacked supernatural theism. Such a repudiation would by implication constitute an attack on the official Christian or Muslim religion as well, and subject the Jews who advocated it to charges of atheism and treason.[62]

2. Accordingly, it was not until political religious freedom was attained by Jews that they were able to reject Orthodoxy and create new religions. By the end of the nineteenth century, significant numbers of Jews possessed political religious freedom. This was due to revolutionary changes in the eighteenth and nineteenth centuries respecting political religious freedom in countries to which Jews were native or had emigrated. Governments came into power that either instituted the principle of separation of religion (church) and state,[63] which ipso facto granted Jews political religious freedom, or, if an official religion was retained, granted political religious freedom to all their inhabitants regardless of their beliefs.[64] Hence, secure in their political religious freedom, large numbers of Jews in the nineteenth century could, if other relevant factors warranted the decision,[65] discard Orthodoxy and develop new religions without fear of government reprisal.

Economic conditions: Two factors were of particular importance in the nineteenth century in contributing to the development of new religions by Jews.

1. It is a fact of religious history that persons who live in poverty without adequate food, clothing, and shelter, who suffer from the diseases of poverty, and who have no hope that their circumstances can be improved by human and natural means, are more likely to follow religions based upon faith in supernatural forces, messianism, and the hereafter than are people who are affluent. In the course of the nineteenth century, the economic status of Jews generally improved dramatically over that which it had been. Moreover, even individual Jews who did not prosper by and large did not despair. For circumstances were such that there were bright expectations for them if they persevered, and at the very least there was the prospect of prosperity for their children. The poverty that induced

oppressive hopelessness and helped fuel belief in Orthodoxy's promise of a supernatural good life in the Messianic Era and the hereafter was substantially relieved. Consequently, as the economic conditions of Jews improved, so do we find increased rejection of Orthodoxy and an openness toward new religions.

2. Antagonistic economic structures, those whose work times are at variance with the Orthodox ceremonial calendar, exact a substantial financial penalty from those who observe the Orthodox holy days. To illustrate: there is no more important holy day in Orthodoxy than the Sabbath; that Yahveh commanded its observance is among Orthodoxy's basic tenets. Testifying to the importance of the Sabbath is the fact that the punishment for its violation is death,[66] although Orthodoxy in our time is without the political power to exact this penalty. Prohibition of all work is a basic principle among the rules governing observance of the Sabbath.[67] This means, since the Orthodox Sabbath begins on Friday evening at sundown and concludes at sunset on Saturday, that no Orthodox Jew may tend to financial matters or labor in any way during this period. In the nineteenth century, when enormous numbers of Jews left the ghettos of Europe, they found that unlike the ghetto's economic structures, whose work times were congenial to Orthodox ceremonial life, the mainstream economic structures of the countries to which they came were antagonistic. Particularly onerous financially was observance of the Sabbath, since Saturday was generally the most important day for trade in the kinds of commerce in which Jews were engaged in the nineteenth century. As a consequence, Jews were forced to think very seriously about the truth of Orthodoxy and the validity of its ceremonial structure. They might have gone along with Orthodoxy through inertia and by rote had it fit their lives, but a religion that occasioned financial penalties (and seriously interfered with social relationships, as pointed out below) could not be accepted without serious thought. It makes little sense to suffer for a religion in which

one does not believe. Accordingly, in the nineteenth century many Jews became highly sensitized to whatever arguments or evidence there was that indicated Orthodoxy was false. This is not to say that these Jews rejected Orthodox observance for economic and social reasons while really believing Orthodoxy true, but that the former's negative economic and social effects heightened their awareness of and receptivity to the many reasons that existed to support the conclusion it was false.

Social Conditions: By social conditions is meant the broad spectrum of interpersonal forces that influence interactions between the individual and group. Inevitably, these forces are many and varied so that the ones described represent the most basic rather than a survey of the whole.

1. Until the nineteenth century, the great majority of Jews lived in political or social ghettos,[68] and their social lives, except in rare instances, were confined to relationships with other Jews. With the nineteenth century's gradual decrease in political and economic anti-Semitism there appeared a decrease in social anti-Semitism as well. No change affected the social life of the Jews more powerfully than did lessened social anti-Semitism. Personal relationships with non-Jews brought membership in non-Jewish society and organizational life, and introduced Jews to new ideas, values, and cultural activities. Orthodoxy could now be seen from vantage points which gave them a different perspective on the truth, validity, and relevance of Orthodox belief and practice.

2. In the political and social ghettos, Orthodox Judaism, administered and enforced by Orthodox rabbis and powerful communal leaders, was the quasi-official religion. Since Jews in a ghetto were almost entirely restricted in their social lives to relations with other Jews, great pressure could be brought

upon individual Jews by threatening to sever these relationships. Accordingly, violations or rejections of Orthodoxy in the ghetto were punished by Orthodox rabbis by excommunicating and ostracizing the transgressor. A Jew who was excommunicated, and who by reason of political or social anti-Semitism was compelled to live among Orthodox Jews, was a human being isolated. No one other than her or his immediate family could speak to or have commercial dealings with the person, or even come near the person physically. Excommunication was the standard weapon employed against Jews who rejected Orthodoxy and proposed new religions.[69] As the nineteenth century progressed and political and social anti-Semitism lessened, Jews increasingly developed personal relationships with non-Jews. Thus the once fearsome threat by the Orthodox leadership of excommunication and its resulting isolation faded into insignificance. In this way still another obstacle to the rejection of Orthodoxy and the development of new religions by Jews was removed.[70]

3. Orthodox Jewish practices, whatever their avowed religious purpose,[71] have the practical effect of setting apart Jews from non-Jews. The dietary laws, which prescribe the kinds of foods an Orthodox Jew is permitted to eat, provide a particularly good example of this point. Basic among the acts that strengthen human relationships is partaking of food together. Since non-Jews, practically speaking, cannot satisfy the dietary laws, Jews who follow these rules are unable to break bread with them. The resulting severe social limitations produced by the dietary laws and numerous other Orthodox regulations in the non-ghetto world of the nineteenth century, where Jews and non-Jews had more and more interests in common, insistently raised for Jews the question of the truth and validity of Orthodox Judaism, disposing many of them to give a careful hearing to arguments that were brought against it.

Cultural conditions: Although discussed separately, the following three points are organically related.

1. Taking the term "culture" in its broad sense, the culture of Jews prior to the nineteenth century was one that supported the concepts and practices of Orthodox Judaism. Time was measured by the Orthodox Jewish calendar, with workdays, holidays, and vacation periods determined by the holy days and festivals of Orthodoxy. The everyday language of Jews was Yiddish or Ladino,[72] whose vocabularies, with their considerable Hebrew content, possess a pronounced bias toward Orthodox notions, and separates their users from non-Jews. Music was primarily the music of the synagogue, with words provided by the Orthodox liturgy or Orthodox pietism. Literature for adults and children consisted either of stories from or based on the Bible and Talmud. Painting and sculpture were generally not pursued, owing to the Orthodox prohibition against fashioning images that might be used for idol worship. Accordingly, the culture of Jews prior to the nineteenth century could not have been more congenial to Orthodox Judaism. In the nineteenth century, however, Jews moved in ever greater numbers into cultures that were at best neutral but mostly antagonistic to Orthodoxy. Workdays, holidays, and vacation periods were so determined by civil calendars that the Orthodox calendar played little part in determining the basic temporal events in Jews' lives. Yiddish and Ladino were discarded as Jews became acculturated. They replaced these languages with the vernacular or native languages of the countries in which they resided, languages utterly indifferent to Orthodox concepts and practices. And once becoming acquainted with the literature and fine arts of Western culture, Jews quickly entered in large numbers into the mainstream of Western artistic creativity. The upshot of all this was to take away from Orthodoxy the cultural support it had enjoyed among Jews prior to the nineteenth century. Indeed, within a short time, many Jews brought up in the antagonistic Western

culture found Orthodox beliefs and practices foreign to their view of the world.

2. The curriculum of schools almost all Jews attended prior to the nineteenth century consisted of works that were fundamental to Orthodoxy and expounded its concepts. These were mainly the Bible (as interpreted by Orthodox commentators), the Talmud, and medieval expositions and codifications of the Talmud. Adults who continued their education were taught the same subjects. Moreover, the schools also enforced observance of Orthodox Jewish practices. (The humanities and sciences, except privately and in very rare cases, were not taught.) Such restrictive education naturally furthered belief in Orthodox Judaism, particularly since it began in childhood when people are most trusting, impressionable, and vulnerable. By the end of the nineteenth century, however, the great majority of Jews attended secular schools or received formal instruction in secular studies. This destroyed the monopoly of Orthodox Jewish teachings by introducing Jews en masse to competing, contradictory, and alternative concepts, historiographies, and *Weltanschauungen* current in the general culture.

3. One element of conflict between Orthodox Judaism and Western culture bears special mention: the status of women in Orthodox Judaism is significantly inferior to that of men. Two items from the Orthodox rules regarding divorce will suffice to illustrate this. One is that a husband can divorce his wife, but a wife cannot divorce her husband. This means that only when the husband wants a divorce can a marriage be dissolved; if the wife wants a divorce and the husband refuses to give her one she has no power to initiate proceedings. The other item is that in Orthodoxy there is no Enoch Arden law, namely, a statute providing for divorce and remarriage on the basis of an unexplained absence of the husband for a prescribed period of time (usually seven years). Moreover, Orthodoxy does not recognize civil divorce. Accordingly, should a woman whose husband will not grant her an Orthodox divorce, or one whose husband has been absent without

explanation for whatever time the civil law requires, obtain a
civil divorce or other legal dissolution of the marriage and
then remarry, she is regarded by Orthodox law as an adul-
teress. These rules regarding marriage and divorce, which are
among the basic tenets of Orthodoxy, clearly have calamitous
consequences for the women they affect. With society's gradually developing awareness in the nineteenth century of the
moral right of women to equality, the severe disabilities they
suffered under Orthodoxy raised serious doubts among many
Jews regarding its moral values, and opened them to arguments against its truth.

Intellectual conditions: The new conditions described above
encountered by Jews in the nineteenth century—political, economic, social, and cultural—produced an environment that
moved Jews to question seriously the truth of Orthodox Judaism, and heightened their receptivity to reasons for rejecting it.
Moreover, it is most doubtful that without those conditions
present, a new mass religion of Jews could be established.[73]
Nevertheless, it is evident that the mere fact that an environment
is antagonistic to a religion does not mean the religion is false. It
is necessary to deal with a religion on its merits, rejecting its
essential beliefs directly on the basis of relevant refutations of
their credibility. Such refutations appear in the intellectual conditions enumerated below, which may be summarized as having
had several major thrusts: rejection of Orthodoxy's method of
studying its basic texts, rebuttal of the evidence Orthodoxy employs to prove its truth, intuitive rejection of Orthodoxy, refutation of theological arguments historically put forth to corroborate
the theology of Orthodoxy, and the repudiation of fundamental
values and rituals taught by Orthodoxy's essential doctrines.

1. The basic evidence necessary to establish the truth of Orthodox Judaism is the Pentateuch. If the Pentateuch is false, in
   whole or in part, both the basic evidence for the truth of
   Orthodoxy and one of its essential beliefs are false, and Ortho-

doxy, therefore, is refuted. The obvious way, therefore, to determine whether Orthodoxy is true is to inquire into the truth of the Pentateuch. The traditional method employed by Jews in investigating the Pentateuch was to accept its truth before undertaking the study, a method that may be termed *faith-before-inquiry.* Faith-before-inquiry, as its name implies, is the opposite of *faith-after-inquiry,* the method whereby a belief is accepted as true only after investigation, and then only if the investigation produces evidence for its truth. Persons who did not employ the faith-before-inquiry method, according to Orthodoxy, could not properly comprehend and judge the Pentateuch.[74] Moreover, Orthodoxy maintained that it is blasphemy and heresy at any time to doubt or suspend judgment regarding the Pentateuch's truth, which would be necessary if a faith-after-inquiry method were used, since assent to the Pentateuch's truth could not be given until the Pentateuch had first been analyzed and evaluated.

Inasmuch as Jewish education was dominated by Orthodox Jews before the nineteenth century, Jews for centuries were imbued from childhood on with the faith-before-inquiry method of pentateuchal study. As Jewish Bible scholars in the nineteenth century became acquainted through secular education with the methodology of the physical and social sciences, many discarded the faith-before-inquiry method of Orthodoxy for the standard faith-after-inquiry method of scientific scholarship. Broadly described, the faith-after-inquiry method entails embarking upon an inquiry in a neutral state of mind, that is, without presuppositions. Such a study suspends judgment during the inquiry regarding the truth of the notion being investigated, weighs the evidence for and against the notion objectively, and bases a judgment regarding the notion's truth or falsity on the evidence. If the evidence supports the notion, it is judged true and merits faith; if the evidence weighs against the proposition, it is judged false; and if there is no evidence for the notion, it is judged meaningless. The acceptance of the scientific method in investigating the

Pentateuch—a method often termed "higher criticism"[75]—
leads to conclusions fundamentally different from those of
Orthodox belief with respect to the Pentateuch's authorship,
meaning, purpose, and history (see below, paragraph 2,b).
The Talmud also was subjected to scientific analysis, and
here, too, the conclusions regarding its nature differed radically from Orthodox belief. Scientific method, in which faith
was given to the Pentateuch and Talmud only after objective
examination of their contents, provided Jews with their primary intellectual tool for the rejection of Orthodoxy.

2. The evidence for the truth of Orthodoxy in the nineteenth
century was (as it is today) twofold: the dixit evidence of
tradition and the Pentateuch. Tradition attests to the truth of
the Pentateuch for persons living after the generation of
Moses, and the Pentateuch, as interpreted by Orthodoxy,
attests directly to the truth of Orthodox belief. Without entering into the details of the research involved, nineteenth century scientific scholarship may be said to have revealed the
following.

   a. Regarding tradition:

      i. Tradition, in the case of Orthodoxy, consists above all
      in members of one generation handing down the Penta-
      teuch to members of a succeeding generation with the
      assurance that it is true.[76] Yet no person living in the
      nineteenth century could (or can any person today)
      prove that they had received their testimony that the
      Pentateuch is true from a chain of persons stretching
      back to Moses every one of whom was incapable of
      making an error. Given the nature of tradition as oral
      transmission, and the millennia over which information
      had to travel from one generation to the next by word
      of mouth, tradition had to be rejected as evidence of the
      validity of the Pentateuch. In short, before tradition
      could serve as evidence for the truth of the Pentateuch,
      evidence was first required to show that tradition itself
      was true.

ii. The Talmud is a primary source for the view that a tradition exists testifying to the truth of the Pentateuch.[77] Scientific talmudic scholarship, however, impugned the Talmud's reliability as a record of historical fact. By comparison with authenticated contemporary records, and through internal analysis, the Talmud's ostensible historical reports were found to be unreliable, serving in large measure as propaganda for Pharisaic (early Orthodox) belief.

b. Regarding the Pentateuch:

i. The Pentateuch, upon scientific examination, emerged as a work quite the opposite of that which Orthodoxy declared it to be. For Orthodoxy, every word of the Pentateuch issued directly from Yahveh, the creator God of the universe, by means of a verbal revelation to Moses. Thus the Pentateuch had one author, Yahveh; it was written within a single period of time, the years of Moses' prophethood; and it was, therefore, theologically uniform and self-consistent. Higher criticism, however, came to contrary views, which may be summarized thusly. The Pentateuch is, first of all, not a verbal revelation from a creator God of the universe, but a human work. Moreover, it was authored not by one human, but by many, and, in addition, was subjected to frequent editing and reediting. Furthermore, the various authors and redactors lived in different periods of time extending over at least a thousand years, and often their theological viewpoints differed. As a human composite from antiquity, therefore, the Pentateuch is not an infallible, uniform, and self-consistent work, but one that contains numerous errors, incoherencies, and contradictions. Accordingly, the foundation stone of Orthodoxy, that the Pentateuch is an infallible and eternally valid work revealed by an infinitely perfect creator God, was judged by many Jews in the nineteenth century to be false, refuted by the evidence disclosed by higher criticism.

ii. We may add this further point with respect to the Talmud. As stated earlier, the Talmud and the Pentateuch together comprise, according to Orthodoxy, the full revelation communicated infallibly to Moses. Since the claim by Orthodoxy that the Talmud is infallible revelation is based solely upon the Pentateuch, refuting the latter invalidates the former. Consequently, there is no need to provide an independent refutation of the Talmud once the Pentateuch's infallibility is taken as disproved. Nevertheless, it should be pointed out that the Talmud's infallible revelatory status was convincingly undermined by nineteenth century scientific scholarship. If the Talmud were, as Orthodoxy claimed, the work of a single author, the creator God of the universe, we would expect it to be uniform, self-consistent, and inerrant. Yet scientific analysis of the texts of the Talmud provided compelling evidence that it had been composed in basically the same manner as the Pentateuch, by human authors writing over many centuries. And, like the Pentateuch, the Talmud exhibits profound internal contradictions reflecting the changing ideological, economic, and political conditions of the different times in which these authors lived. Such evidence persuaded significant numbers of Jews in the nineteenth century, particularly scholarly and clerical leaders, that the belief the Talmud is verbal revelation is false.

3. It would be unrealistic to think that the majority of Jews who in the nineteenth century regarded Orthodoxy as false did so on the basis of scientific inquiry into the Pentateuch and the Talmud. They possessed neither the requisite knowledge of nor training in scientific and historical textual analysis. Nevertheless, they rejected Orthodoxy. The reason for this is to be found in their *reality-view.* A reality-view is defined as comprising the total range of notions that a person accepts as true. The point at which a person's ability to give credence to notions stops is the *reality-view boundary.* The notions in-

cluded within a reality-view and those beyond its boundary are arrived at in different ways, some consciously, through philosophic and scientific analysis, some nonconsciously, from general environmental transmission, and still others intuitively. The point is that one need not be an academically trained thinker to decide a religion is false. A person can make the judgment that a religion is false simply by feeling or intuiting that one or more of its essential beliefs are false, without technical analysis of the religion's entire structure.[78] Increasing numbers of nineteenth century Jews found essential Orthodox beliefs to be beyond their reality-view boundary, and therefore, false, even though these Jews had not examined these beliefs thoroughly in a philosophic or scientific manner.

4. Four final points respecting intellectual conditions in the nineteenth century that challenged the faith of Jews in Orthodoxy require mention.

  a. In the history of philosophy, from Aristotle to the time of Hume and Kant, three proofs for the existence of a deity were widely held: the cosmological, teleological, and ontological arguments.[79] It is important to understand the status and significance of these three proofs, although it is unnecessary to enter into details of their reasoning here.

    First, these "philosophic" proofs were the equivalent of what today would be regarded as "scientific" proofs. No use was made of supernaturalism, such as revelation and miracles, in these proofs. They were based upon empirical experience and reasoning, or upon reasoning alone.[80] No philosophers subscribed to every proof, but the greatest philosophers and finest minds of the Western world before Hume and Kant accepted at least one of these proofs.

    Second, the philosophic proofs were considered by those who proposed them to be absolutely certain and logically compelling to every mind capable of comprehending them.

    Third, and this must be emphasized, none of these proofs demonstrated the truth of the concepts of deity prescribed by such religions as Orthodox Judaism, Roman Catholicism, or Sunni Islam. To illustrate why this is so: Orthodoxy, Catholicism, and Sunni all require a theistic deity who exercises miraculous providence and supernaturally reveals his desires to humans, but none of the three proofs establishes the existence of a miracle-working or self-revealing deity, still less any of the unique characteristics that make each of these religions' concepts of God fundamentally different from the others. What the philosophic proofs did accomplish for these religions was to show that the finest human minds, employing purely natural faculties and engaged in philosophic or scientific inquiry, the most disciplined and logical form of human reasoning, demonstrated that there existed a deity of some kind. This provided impressive ancillary evidence for the religions, although each of them maintained that it was necessary to resort to the unique supernatural, infallible revelation each claimed to possess in order to attain a correct understanding of the deity's true nature.

By the nineteenth century, the cosmological, teleological, and ontological arguments for the existence of a deity were generally considered by philosophers and scientists to have been refuted by the eighteenth century thinkers David Hume and Immanuel Kant. Moreover, no other proofs were ever again accepted by acknowledged leading thinkers as compelling to every competent human mind, although individuals might find one or the other of these arguments personally persuasive.[81] In addition, during this period, the position became clearly established that no concept of deity plays a part in or is relevant in any way to scientific inquiry and knowledge.[82] Consequently, whatever auxiliary support human knowledge acquired through philosophy and science might have given to Orthodoxy in the Middle Ages had already evaporated when Jews in the nineteenth century once again became aware of and entered into the mainstream of Western thought.[83]

b. Human beings are dependent for the continuation and quality of their physical existence upon such necessities as food and health. According to Orthodoxy and other supernatural religions, the source of these necessities is the deity, who in his omniscience and omnipotence exercises providence over humankind. Those who obey the deity are rewarded by the bestowal of life's necessities; those who disobey are punished by being deprived of them. Specifically, in Orthodoxy, the deity is Yahveh who revealed commandments to Moses that all Jews must obey. Those who obey these commandments are rewarded with life's necessities; those who disobey them are punished by starvation and disease.[84] The only way in which those who have disobeyed Yahveh can receive his forgiveness and once again obtain life's necessities is to atone for their sins in the manner prescribed and provided by Orthodox belief and ritual. For almost two millennia, most Jews accepted the Orthodox view of the way in which life's necessities are attained. They knew no explanation for starvation and disease other than Yahveh's supernatural punishment, and saw no way to overcome them except to beg his forgiveness in the manner prescribed by Orthodoxy. Consequently, Orthodoxy was deemed generally by Jews to be absolutely vital to the quality of their lives and even to their very survival. Renouncing Orthodoxy would have meant casting away the only course of action able to be taken in times of distress, and the abandonment of all hope for dealing with bodily suffering. With the rapid growth of science and technology in the nineteenth century, Jews became aware of an alternative method for dealing with starvation and disease: the acquisition of a scientific understanding of the laws of nature and the application of it to technological innovation directed to the solution of human ills. According to science and technology, starvation and disease had no relationship to the adherence to Orthodoxy. When science and technology developed methods to improve the food supply and combat disease, there was an increase in food and health, and when science and technology fell short, there was not. Moreover, even when science and technology did fall short, their rapid advance and increasing success promised that their procedures offered the only concrete and realistic prospect for bettering human life in the future. Consequently, as the efficacy of science and technology burgeoned, the faith of great numbers of Jews in the Orthodox belief regarding supernatural providence weakened, and inasmuch as this belief is essential to Orthodoxy's truth, serious doubts arose among many respecting the correctness of Orthodoxy itself.

c. Psychiatry was in its infancy toward the end of the nineteenth century, but it was a powerful force in the Western world in the twentieth. Before the advent of psychiatry, there was for most persons no way other than through supernatural religions to understand and cope with hallucination, delusions, anxiety, depression, and other painful psychic states.[85] With the rise of psychiatry, however, and psychoanalysis in particular, naturalistic methods became available to explain and deal with these conditions. Psychiatry gradually proved itself to most Jews to be more efficacious in dealing with mental and emotional disturbances than supernatural religion. So here again, faith in the validity of Orthodoxy was weakened.[86]

d. Improving the material aspects of human life and providing a naturalistic means for dealing with painful mental and emotional states were not the only ways in which science, technology, and psychiatry produced a threat to Orthodox belief. They also pointed to an alternative world view: *naturalism*. Naturalism denies that any events or objects have a miraculous origin, cause, or explanation, and maintains that laws and explanations verified by ordinary and repeatable human sense and introspective experiences are adequate to account for all events and objects. The appeal of naturalism was based not only on the achievements of science, technology, and psychiatry, but also on the failure of supernatural religions like Orthodoxy to provide credible evidence of miraculous intervention by a theistic God in the affairs of humankind although such providence clearly has been and is sorely needed.[87] As a result, naturalism has been widely subscribed to among Jews, especially by academicians, scientists, and other intellectual groups.

Correction of Misconceptions Regarding the Present Religious Situation of Jews

Having provided the necessary groundwork, we can now turn to our basic task: correcting the three prevalent, fundamental misconceptions enumerated earlier regarding the religious life of contemporary Jews.

Correction of First Misconception

The first misconception is that all contemporary Jews subscribe to one religion. This notion is easily seen to be erroneous by comparing the essential beliefs of Orthodox Judaism with their corresponding beliefs in Reform Judaism.[88] It will be unnecessary to compare all the essential beliefs of Orthodoxy with those of Reform since religions are different even if they are nonidentical with respect to just one essential belief.[89] We will therefore compare only a selection, with the Orthodox beliefs followed by those in Reform that correspond to them. Inasmuch as the comparisons demonstrate clearly that these essential beliefs of Orthodoxy and Reform are nonidentical, the conclusion is evident that the two are different religions, and inasmuch as they are both religions to which Jews subscribe, the point can be clearly established that contemporary Jews divide into groups that adhere to different religions.

1. *Orthodox belief:* Yahveh, the creator God of the universe, communicated the Pentateuch to Moses by verbal revelation. The Pentateuch is therefore infallible and authoritative for all Jews, who, consequently, are obligated to obey absolutely its commandments.

   Reform belief: The Pentateuch is not a verbal revelation; accordingly, it is neither infallible nor authoritative for Jews.

   Comment: The Reform belief is apparent in these statements issued by two Reform rabbinic conferences:

   ". . . [T]he Bible (reflects) the primitive ideas of its own age. . . ."

   "We recognize in the Mosaic legislation[90] a system of training the Jewish people for its mission during its national life in Palestine, and today we accept as binding only its moral laws, and maintain only such ceremonies as elevate and sanctify our lives, but reject all such as are not adapted to the views and habits of modern civilization."[91]

   "We hold that all such Mosaic and rabbinical laws as regulate diet, priestly purity, and dress originated in ages and under the spiritual influence of ideas entirely foreign to our present mental and spiritual state. They fail to impress the modern Jew with a spirit of priestly holiness; their observance in our days is apt rather to obstruct than to further modern spiritual elevation."[92]

2. *Orthodox belief:* The Talmud was revealed to Moses through a verbal revelation, and it is, therefore, authoritative for and obligatory upon all Jews.

   Reform belief: The Talmud was not revealed through a verbal revelation; thus it is neither authoritative nor obligatory for Jews.

   Comment: The Reform position is explicitly stated in the following pronouncement issued by a Reform rabbinic conference:

   "From the standpoint of Reform Judaism, the whole post-

Biblical and patristic literature, including the Talmud, casuists, responses, and commentaries is, and can be considered as nothing more nor less than 'religious literature'. . . . [T]he more the conditions and environments of our modern life force it upon us, the more persistently we have to assert that our relations in all religious matters are in no way authoritatively and finally determined by any portion of our post-Biblical and patristic literature."[93]

3. *Orthodox belief:* The Yahvistic concept of deity that appears in the Pentateuch is Yahveh's supernatural, infallible revelation of his own nature. This Yahvistic concept is therefore absolutely and eternally true, and no change in this concept may ever be made by humans.

Reform belief: The Yahvistic concept of a miracle-working deity that appears in the Pentateuch has no substantiation inasmuch as the Pentateuch is a fallible, human document replete with errors and primitive notions. Accordingly, Reform Jews have a right to reject the pentateuchal view of Yahveh and develop new concepts of deity as history progresses.

Comment: The Reform view is reflected in the following statements of the Central Conference of American Rabbis:

"We hold that the modern discoveries of scientific researches in the domain of nature and history are not antagonistic to the doctrines of Judaism, the Bible reflecting the primitive ideas of its own age, and at times clothing its conception of Divine Providence and Justice dealing with man in miraculous narrative."[94]

"We recognize in Judaism a progressive religion, ever striving to be in accord with the postulates of reason."[95]

"We hold that Judaism presents the highest conception of the God-idea as taught in our Holy Scriptures and developed and spiritualized by the Jewish teachers, in accordance with the moral and philosophical progress of their respective ages."[96]

Correction of Second Misconception

The second misconception, which is based on the first, is that the one contemporary religion of Jews is the Orthodox Jewish Cognate Complex, that is, Orthodox Judaism or one of several variations essentially similar to Orthodoxy. This notion is shown to be false by the evidence presented above, which demonstrates that Reform Judaism is a different religion from Orthodoxy. Since the two are different religions, Reform cannot be an essentially similar variation of Orthodoxy. Therefore, seeing that some Jews are adherents of Orthodoxy, others of Reform, the Orthodox Jewish Cognate Complex is not the one contemporary religion of Jews.[97]

Correction of Third Misconception

The third misconception is the notion that the most general fundamental principle underlying the contemporary religious life of Jews is belief in a supernatural covenant between Jews and a theistic deity. To deal with this misconception, it is necessary to have clearly in mind the nature of the supernatural covenant that constitutes an essential belief of Orthodox Judaism.

A covenant, in general terms, is a binding agreement or contract between two (or more) parties in which each promises to perform some action or actions in consideration of the other (or others) performing some action (or actions). According to Orthodoxy, there is such a covenant, which will be referred to as the Orthodox Covenant, between Jews and Yahveh.[98,99] The terms of the Orthodox Covenant, broadly stated, are that Yahveh promises to be the god of the Jews, that is, to exercise a special providence over them, in return for their promise to be his people, that is, their promise to obey the commandments Yahveh has laid down in the Pentateuch and the Talmud. Since, according to Orthodoxy, the Pentateuch and Talmud are verbal revelation, it is absolutely authoritative for all Jews, who are obligated to obey every one of the commandments the Pentateuch and Talmud contain.

As we have seen, however, Reform denies that the Pentateuch and Talmud constitute verbal revelation, maintaining rather that they are fallible and unauthoritative, so that Jews are not obligated to obey their commandments. It is clear, then, that by denying the authoritative and obligatory nature of the commandments in the Pentateuch and Talmud, and by rejecting practically all of them, Reform rejects the terms of the Orthodox Covenant, and, consequently, repudiates the Orthodox Covenant itself.

Reform Community Has No Covenant With A Deity

We may, then, raise this question: does the Reform Jewish community have grounds for maintaining that it has a different covenant with a theistic deity, which consists of terms other than those of the Sinaitic covenant or Orthodox Covenant? The answer is that Reform does not. Neither a description nor evidence of the terms of any "Reform Covenant" has ever been given.[100] Without terms there can be no possibility of a covenant, inasmuch as a covenant is nothing other than its terms (that is, the nature of a covenant is "ability to be kept," and no one can keep a covenant whose terms are nonexistent). A covenant without terms is a self-contradiction.

The Ratio-Moral Authority Principle

By the foregoing analysis and comparison of Orthodox Judaism with Reform Judaism, the fact has been established that there is more than one religion followed by contemporary Jews. We must hasten to add, however, that by choosing Orthodoxy and Reform to illustrate that there are a multiplicity of religions among Jews, there was no intention of implying that these are the only two. In point of fact, there are a number of religions in addition to Orthodoxy and Reform to which contemporary Jews adhere. Among those that are formally institutionalized are Conservative Judaism, Reconstructionist Judaism, and Polydox Judaism; and there are a number of others that are informally organized.

The diversity of religions among Jews that emerged in the nineteenth century, after centuries of almost total adherence by Jews to Orthodox Judaism, prompts the question whether some underlying general principle, consciously or subconsciously, is operative here. The answer that suggests itself is that there is such a principle: the *ratio-moral authority principle,* which consists of two parts:[101]

1. Authority can be exercised justifiably by one member or group of members over other members of a religious community only if the community possesses an objectively verifiable verbal revelation in which a theistic deity grants to those who exercise authority the right to dictate to other members the beliefs and practices they must follow. Such authority is rational and moral in that it is sanctioned by the creator God of the universe. A community that possesses ratio-moral authority properly takes an authoritarian and orthodox form.

2. In a religious community that explicitly or implicitly denies the existence of an objectively verifiable verbal revelation in which a theistic deity grants to some member (or members) of the community the right to exercise authority over other members, the exercise of such authority is unjustified and should not be attempted. But if it is attempted, it is rightly rejected and disregarded. Such a religious community, consequently, properly takes one of the polydox forms.[102]

Jews Have Followed The Ratio-Moral Authority Principle

Jews, however diverse their religions may have been, have historically followed, consciously or subconsciously, the ratio-moral authority principle. Hence we find that the Orthodox community, which is authoritarian and orthodox, affirms unequivocally that it possesses an objectively verifiable verbal revelation that grants it authority over all Jews. On the other hand, each of the religious communities of Jews that emerged in the nineteenth and twentieth centuries has rejected, explicitly or implicitly, the existence of an objectively verifiable verbal revelation, and each can be characterized as having followed the ratio-moral authority principle and possessing a polydox form. Taking, then, three formally institutionalized religions of contemporary Jews, in addition to Reform, we find the following:

1. Conservative Judaism is a de facto and latent polydoxy. Although Conservatism has tended to present itself as identical to Orthodox Judaism, it has been clear from Conservatism's inception that it is a de facto polydoxy. Its members have by and large felt free to believe what they wish to, and they keep whatever observances they choose. In the last several decades, it has become increasingly clear that Conservatism is also a latent polydoxy. If the Mosaic revelation is believed to be verbal revelation, then it must be followed absolutely and completely. Yet in two areas, Conservatism has clearly rejected commandments of the Mosaic revelation regarding the observance of the Sabbath and the status of women.[103] The necessary implication of the Conservative community's rejection of the Mosaic revelation as verbal revelation is that the community has no justifiable base upon which to exercise authority, and is, therefore, a latent polydoxy.[104]

2. Although Reconstructionist Judaism places great emphasis upon ethnicism, it also sets forth a religion. This religion constitutes a latent and de facto polydoxy. Belief in a verbal revelation that comes to humans through a supernatural act from a theistic deity has been rejected by Reconstructionists from the start. Most prominent Reconstructionist thinkers have been theological naturalists who have rejected all supernaturalism, including supernatural concepts of deity.[105]

3. Polydox Judaism, as its name indicates, is a polydoxy, explicitly affirming the Freedom Covenant as its fundamental principle.[106]

Relevance to Christianity

The foregoing analysis has relevance beyond the contemporary

religious life of Jews. The nineteenth and twentieth centuries
have also been periods in which change has affected other religious communities, notably Christian ones. Conditions basically
similar to those that confronted Orthodox Jews and resulted in
the emergence of new Jewish religions have challenged Orthodox
and fundamentalist Christians and given rise to new religions
among Christians.[107] Probably inevitable in the process of emergent religions evolving from matrix religions is the considerable
confusion, ideological as well as emotional, that arises respecting
the basic character of the emergent religions.[108] Three points
from the analysis presented above can contribute to the clarification of the natures and statuses of these emergent religions.

1. When a religion emerges from a matrix religion, the former
    will as a rule show some resemblance to the latter, be it in
    the area of belief, liturgy, ritual, symbolism, or names. Such
    similarities understandably constitute a basic cause of confu-
    sion over whether the two religions are the same or different.
    Thus the criterion laid down above for determining whether
    two or more religions are different from one another, namely,
    if one or more of their essential beliefs are nonidentical,[109] is
    vital to clarifying the relationship between matrix and emergent
    religions.
2. No more bitter controversies have taken place historically
    among religions than those between members of a matrix and
    emergent religion. Foremost among the reasons for this is
    that they see themselves as adherents of the same religion
    contending for the same ideational and community territory
    rather than regarding themselves as adherents of two different
    religions. Thus each group condemns the other as sinful and
    heretical. Once the members of the matrix and emergent reli-
    gions realize that they are adherents of two different religions
    with, consequently, two different territories, the intensity of
    feeling between them can abate. Moderate relations generally
    prevail today between members of different religious com-
    munities, and one can hope such relations will replace the

intensely negative ones that exist between warring factions of the same religious community.

3. The two major categories into which religions fall, judged on the basis of concepts fundamental to all religions, revelation and authority, are orthodox and polydox. Whether the religion of a community is properly one or the other is critical to the rights of the community's members and the morality of its authority structure. Accordingly, it is of essential importance to determine clearly whether a community's religion is orthodox or polydox. This can be accomplished by applying the ratio-moral authority principle to an analysis of the community's concepts of revelation and authority.

Notes

1. The term *modern* will be used to refer to the 19th and 20th centuries. When the term *contemporary* is employed, it refers to the present at the time of this writing. Accordingly, the contemporary period is included in the modern age (or period) and constitutes the modern age's latest phase.

2. This point has been alluded to above, p. 75.

3. Prominently placed among the ostensible essentially similar variations of Orthodox Judaism are Reform Judaism and Conservative Judaism.

4. Of course, even with the use of qualifying adjectives such as "Orthodox" and "Reform," many persons are still misled by the use of the same term "Judaism" in the phrases "Orthodox Judaism" and "Reform Judaism" into thinking that the two religions are essentially similar when, in fact, they are essentially dissimilar; see pp. 117 ff.

5. The state of Israel, e.g., recognizes legally the existence of only one Jewish religion, Orthodox Judaism.

6. Sadducean Judaism, of course, is also present in the New Testament, but Pharisaic Judaism has historically been more vivid in the awareness of Christians.

7. The phrase "New Testament Christians" will be used to refer to Christians whose religious beliefs are based upon the New Testament so that if the New Testament were false, their beliefs would be false. "New Testament Christianity" is the religion of New Testament Christians. Roman Catholic and fundamentalist Protestantism are examples of New Testament Christianity. It is conceivable that there should be a Christianity that regards the New Testament as false.

8. Although the Bible is considered to have been fulfilled and transcended by the New Testament, its contents are regarded as having been true revelation since the time they were communicated.

9. *Mutatis mutandis,* the point made in this paragraph applies to Jews living in Muslim countries.

10. Critically, the reason for rejecting Orthodox Judaism is that objective, scientific analysis does not bear out the fundamental principle that the Pentateuch is an infallible work of a single author who is the theistic creator God of the universe.

11. There are a number of reasons for rejecting the Pentateuch on moral grounds. Among them: it condones and supports slavery; it legislates sexism; and it vehemently opposes the religious autonomy of the individual.

12. See M. Maimonides, *The Guide of the Perplexed,* I, 50; cf. of A. J. Reines, "Birth Dogma and Philosophic Religious Faith," *HUCA* XLVI (1975).

13. It need not be a religious or theological proposition to which one gives faith. Faith as the act of assent to the truth of a proposition applies equally to scientific and any other propositions that are accepted as true.

14. Verbal forms of the term faith that will be employed are "to give faith to" or "to faith," which are equivalent to "to believe." Hence, to give faith to, to faith, or to believe a religion is to assent to the truth of the fundamental propositions, tenets, beliefs, or dogmas of the religion.

15. As, e.g., apprehending empirically the Sinaitic revelation or a scientific experiment and comprehending their natures. Aristotle's cosmological argument for the existence of God also illustrates sensation working in combination with reason.

16. As, e.g., the ontological arguments of Descartes and Spinoza.

17. Exodus 19:9-20:19; Deuteronomy 18:15-18. All biblical narratives are cited as illustrations, not because they are regarded as true by the author.

18. A distinction is drawn here between essentially unique events and nonessentially unique events. An event is essentially unique if there is no other event that is regarded as essentially similar to it. Hence once an essentially unique event is past, nothing essentially similar to it can be experienced. An event is nonessentially unique if there occur other events essentially similar to it. Consequently, even though a nonessentially unique event may be past, the evidence it provides can still be obtained from another event that is essentially similar to it. The revelation at Mount Sinai, as described in the Bible, is an essentially unique event. Once past, the evidence it provides cannot be repeated. A given body of water is nonessentially unique so that if a particular body of water no longer exists, one can go to another body of water for whatever evidence the first body of water might have provided. The physical sciences require the concept of nonessentially unique events as do any disciplines that are dependent upon repeatable evidence.

19. To apprehend certain kinds of objective repeatable evidence, particularly in the physical sciences, special skills and instruments are required, but these are themselves naturally attainable by those who seek to observe the evidence.

20. It was the repeatable testability of these arguments that enabled other persons, notably Hume and Kant, to examine and refute them.

21. Objective evidence, as defined above (pp. 86 f.), is not apprehended supernaturally; the process of apprehending objective evidence, whether sensing or reasoning, is always natural. If the apprehending is supernatural, as, e.g., when the senses, imagination, or reason are acted on by a miracle-working deity so that they apprehend visions or the like which impart information not naturally attainable, then the apprehension used for evidence constitutes subjective evidence. For an illustration of supernatural apprehension, see A. J. Reines, *Maimonides and Abrabanel on Prophecy* (Cincinnati, 1970), pp. 118 ff.

22. Psychoanalysis, by this definition, is ultimately based upon subjective evidence.

23. The vision, according to the Bible, provides Abraham with evidence that the god to be known as Yahveh exists, and that there is a covenant between Yahveh and the Hebrews.

24. See below, pp. 170 ff.

25. Hearsay evidence in the law is equivalent to dixit evidence.

26. So the validity of Orthodox Judaism is entirely dependent upon the truth of the Pentateuch (and Talmud); the validity of Roman Catholic and fundamentalist Protestantism upon the truth of the New Testament; and the validity of Islam upon the truth of the Koran. Since the Pentateuch, New Testament, and Koran are all ancient Scriptures, the only evidence for their truth that exists (for someone who does not receive private revelations or intuitions guaranteeing their truth) is that some person or group says they are true, i.e., dixit evidence.

27. Because it is only hearsay, and unable to be verified in any way.

28. A distinction is to be drawn between the "trust" of nonevidential cognitive faith, described in the previous paragraph, and the "trust" of noncognitive truth. In the case of the former, the trust impels the person to assent to the truth of a proposition or belief that, although without evidence, is nonetheless understood or conceived by the person's intellect, as, e.g., "Yahveh, a being possessing certain characteristics, is the creator God of the universe"; in the latter case, the trust is an action that has no conceptualized or known object.

29. From this point, if "noncognitive faith" is meant, the entire phrase will be written out, whereas "cognitive faith" will be referred to simply as "faith."

30. This is not to say that all those who base their view of what is true on the senses and/or reason will arrive at the same conclusions, but nonetheless, that whatever their conclusions may be, they are based upon sensing and/or reasoning.

31. E.g., if a person should have experienced what was taken at the time to be a miraculous encounter with an angel, there would be no way at some later time, if memory should falter, to reexamine the experience to

determine whether it was, in fact, a miraculous encounter, a dream, an illusion, or a hallucination.

32. See, e.g., J. Albo, *Sefer Ha-Ikkarim (Book of Principles)*, IV, 44.

33. Unless the person receives a revelation attesting to the truth of the tradition.

34. The terms *Jew, Judaism*, and *Jewish* are employed to refer to persons and religions that are at times more accurately referred to as Hebrew and Israelite. This accords with general usage today and to do otherwise might confuse some readers. The terms *Jew, Judaism*, and *Jewish* do not appear in the two major parts of the Bible at all, namely, the Pentateuch (Torah) and the Prophets, and have a different meaning today from that which they have where they do rarely appear in the Hagiographa. Hence, strictly speaking, Abraham was a Hebrew, Moses, a Hebrew or Israelite, and the religions of the Pentateuch and Prophets, Hebrew or Israelite religions. The words *Jew, Judaism*, and *Jewish* are relatively late arrivals on the scene of history, probably some time after the fourth century B.C.E.

35. Deuteronomy 4:32-36.

36. It is irrelevant for the purpose of illustration whether the pentateuchal account is true and if there ever was in fact such a religion. The point is that if there ever is an unrepeatable objective evidence religion, it is of this type.

37. *Ibid.*, also Exodus 19:9.

38. Deuteronomy 18:16-18; 34:10-12.

39. *The Guide of the Perplexed*, I, 50.

40. The cosmological argument constituted competent evidence for the existence of a deity, but for a person genuinely to believe in this deity it was necessary to understand the cosmological argument and be convinced of it. The person could not take Maimonides' word for it that the cosmological argument was valid and in this way become a genuine believer.

41. See n. 20.

42. One major disagreement concerned the afterlife: the Sadducees denied the existence of an afterlife; the Pharisees believed in resurrection, retribution, and eternal life.

43. A major reason Sadduceeism could not survive the destruction of the Temple was that its observances centered around the sacrificial cult of the Jerusalem Temple. Once the Temple was destroyed and the Jews were exiled, Sadduceeism disintegrated. Pharisaism, on the other hand, had developed a religion that could be observed in synagogues and through home rituals, which had no need of the Temple, and did not require dwelling in the land of Israel.

44. According to the Pentateuch, Abraham also had non-Jewish descendants (non-Hebrew, to be precise), but Yahveh's covenant with Abraham would only pass to his Jewish (i.e., Hebrew) descendants; Genesis 17:18-21.

45. See above, p. 18, for definition of verbal revelation.

46. Not all the commandments are directed toward every Jew. For example, some commandments are obligatory upon men and not upon women, and vice versa, but every commandment directed toward a Jew is obligatory upon her or him. There are also commandments that Orthodox Jews believe are incumbent upon humankind generally.

47. E.g., the Holocaust, which was a punishment for the widespread rejection or violation of Yahveh's commandments by modern Jews.

48. It is possible to say that there are religions without beliefs; the question is whether such a statement has any meaning. A religion without beliefs, i.e., intelligible propositions, is by its nature unable to be stated, and unable, therefore, to be shown to exist.

49. Such as Orthodox Judaism, Roman Catholicism, or Sunni Islam.

50. Owing to the semantic confusions and obfuscations of religious history, it is not always clear whether religions that have come into existence in different epochs or through different routes of cultural development have identical essential beliefs and constitute, therefore, the same religion. Careful examination and analysis are often required to determine if two ostensibly identical religions are, in fact, the same, and vice versa.

51. Thus Pharisaic Judaism, Rabbinic Judaism, and Orthodox Judaism all constitute the same religion; they share the same essential beliefs while differing with respect to some nonessential beliefs.

52. Any difference at all between the essential beliefs of two religions means they are different religions. E.g., if a religion has four essential beliefs and shares three of these with another religion, but the other religion either lacks the fourth belief, or has another essential belief in place of the fourth, the religions are different religions.

53. By "human history" is meant present ordinary history which in Orthodox Judaism and various kinds of Christianity is understood to come to an end with the coming of the Messiah. See essential belief 8 of Orthodox Judaism on p. 100.

54. I have abstracted these essential beliefs from the Pentateuch and the Talmud.

55. These conditions affected and continue to affect Catholic and fundamentalist Christians as well as Muslims, in much the same way that they affected and still affect Orthodox Jews.

56. See, e.g., Leo Strauss, *Persecution and the Art of Writing* (Glencoe, Il.: Free Press, 1952), pp. 17 ff; also see Maimonides' Introduction to *The Guide of the Perplexed.*

57. Practically speaking, political religious freedom is never absolute. E.g., human sacrifice can be outlawed in a country that is considered as granting its inhabitants religious freedom. The United States may be viewed as a typical country that grants political freedom. *Note that political religious freedom is to be distinguished from polydox religious freedom.* Political religious freedom is that which is granted by the government of a country to those who live in the country; polydox religious freedom is that

which is granted by a religious community to its members (and for that matter, to all other humans).

58. As in medieval Christian and Islamic countries and in a number of countries today. In the Soviet Union, the Russian version of dialectical materialism or Marxism can be considered the official religion.

59. As, e.g., in the present-day Vatican City, or the theocratic system described in the Pentateuch.

60. In antiquity, Jews for the most part lived in "Jewish" countries, but these were theocracies and they did not grant their subjects political religious freedom, i.e., the right to reject without harm the official "Jewish" religion.

61. It goes without saying that anti-Semitism (discrimination against a person fundamentally on the basis that she or he can be construed to have the name "Jew") exacerbated the difficulties encountered by Jews in all the areas enumerated. Thus there was political anti-Semitism, where persons were denied civil rights because they were Jews, i.e., had the name Jew; economic anti-Semitism, where Jews were denied equal economic opportunities; social anti-Semitism, the denial of human relationships and association memberships to Jews; cultural anti-Semitism, the prohibition of Jews from participating in the fine arts and humanities (as well as villification of Jews in literature and theater); and intellectual anti-Semitism, where Jews were denied the right to acquire a competent education in the fields of their choice. Having said this, it must be emphasized that the situation of the majority of non-Jews was often little better than that of Jews. So, e.g., under feudalism, Jews and non-Jews alike were chattel; under marginal economic systems, Jews and non-Jews alike were exploited and impoverished; under aristocratic social and cultural institutions, Jews and non-Jews alike were déclassé; and before modern science and technology, Jews and non-Jews alike died of disease, malnutrition, and other natural disasters that have now been controlled or eliminated. Accordingly, Jews and non-Jews alike accepted belief in supernatural, authoritarian theisms—Orthodox Judaism, Catholic and Protestant Christianities, and various Islamic sects—and conditions such as those which were encountered by most Jews in the nineteenth century, and which challenged their belief in Orthodoxy, also have been encountered by Christians and Muslims and challenged their belief. Many Christians, however, met these conditions earlier than the nineteenth century, and most Muslims have encountered them in the twentieth century.

62. Although Jews are here specifically mentioned, the same holds true for other persons who did not subscribe to the official religions of countries with establishment religious institutions. A major reason so many Jews acquired political religious freedom in the 19th century was the massive emigration to the U.S. during that period from repressive countries such as Russia and Poland.

63. E.g., France and the United States.

64. E.g., England.

65. As those enumerated below.

66. Numbers 15:32-36.

67. There are numerous other holidays in Orthodoxy beside the Sabbath on which work is prohibited: four days each on Pesach and Sukkot, two days each on Rosh Hashanah and Shavuot, and one day on Yom Kippur.

68. Political anti-Semitism is that which is decreed by the law of the land; social anti-Semitism is practiced voluntarily by individuals and organizations. Similarly, a political ghetto is one established by law, whereas a social ghetto is created by individuals. A notorious example of a political ghetto was the Pale of Settlement established in czarist Russia in 1791.

69. Although Spinoza lived in the 17th century, his experience presents a classic illustration of this point; for the conditions he lived under in enlightened Holland were in principle the same as those experienced by most Jews only later, in the 19th century. Spinoza's philosophy, in effect, constitutes a new religion, and one that explicitly repudiates Orthodox Judaism. How much the Orthodox community of Amsterdam, Holland, knew or understood of Spinoza's philosophy is not clear, but they were sufficiently aware of it to see Spinoza as a threat, and excommunicated him.

70. Spinoza's life points this up; since there was no anti-Semitic barrier in Amsterdam to prevent him from relating to non-Jews, he did just that, and enjoyed relationships with non-Jews who were among the finest minds of his time.

71. The fundamental reason for observing the practices, according to Orthodoxy, is that they were revealed and commanded to be observed by Yahveh, the creator God of the universe. Also, the Pentateuch, Orthodoxy's basic revelation, makes it clear that the Jews are a holy community with a special covenantal relation to Yahveh, and that they should, therefore, by the very nature of their chosen status, separate themselves from other religious communities and religionists.

72. Yiddish is a dialect spoken chiefly by Jews in Eastern Europe and the countries to which they have emigrated. Ladino, or Judeo-Spanish, is the language of Jews living in the Balkans and Asia Minor. Hebrew (supplemented by a few Aramaic passages) was the official liturgical language of all Jews until the 19th century.

73. This is so if the historical study of new religions is taken as evidence. No new religion has ever attained a mass following without revolutionary political, economic, social, and cultural changes accompanying its emergence, and supporting its existence.

74. The faith-before-inquiry method is in agreement with Augustine's pronouncement: "Believe in order that you may understand; unless you shall believe, you shall not understand."

75. Aside from religionists, such as Orthodox Jews and Protestant Fundamentalists, who maintain their Scriptures are verbal revelation and literally true, Jewish and Christian scholars alike employ higher criticism at present in studying Scripture.

76. See p. 86.

77. Mishnah Avot 1.1-12.

78. E.g., one who is opposed to slavery might conclude that Orthodoxy is false simply by knowing that, according to the Pentateuch, the deity approves and commands the establishment of the institution of slavery. (Exodus 21:1-6, *et al.*)

79. In the history of theology and philosophy, there have been more than these three arguments offered for the existence of a deity (see, e.g., *The Encyclopedia of Philosophy s.v.* "God, Arguments for the Existence of," [1972 ed.]). The three arguments cited, however, were the principle ones employed by Jews. Medieval Jewish philosophers, notably Maimonides, relied primarily on the cosmological argument. Spinoza is the primary Jewish exponent of the ontological argument. Also, these arguments were the ones primarily advanced by the great Muslim and Christian philosophers.

80. The cosmological and teleological arguments are based upon empirical experience and reasoning; the ontological argument upon reasoning alone.

81. See Chapter VI pp. 155 ff.

82. Aristotle's cosmological argument for the existence of deity as well as his concept of deity, on the other hand, were considered by him to be fundamental elements of scientific knowledge.

83. After a high point of participation in Western philosophy from approximately the 11th through the 14th centuries, Jews were increasingly forbidden access to the general culture so that for several centuries before the nineteenth they were ignorant of developments in Western science and thought. They even became incapable of understanding the technically demanding work of medieval Jewish philosophers such as Maimonides.

84. See, e.g., Deuteronomy 28, *et al.*

85. So, e.g., when Saul, king of Israel, falls into a depression, the Bible says, "Now the spirit of Yahveh had departed from Saul, and an evil spirit from Yahveh terrified him" (I Samuel 16:14-23).

86. Significant numbers of Jewish intellectual and religious leaders have been attracted to the teachings of psychoanalysis. Freud's view, based on psychoanalytic investigation, that supernaturalism in general and theism in particular are fantasies and illusions originating in the unconscious, has had more than a little influence on them. Directly or indirectly, the views of these leaders have filtered through to many persons in the general Jewish population, who, in turn, have had their theological views similarly influenced.

87. The point should be kept in mind that there are meanings of the word God that are not supernatural or theistic. These can be compatible with naturalism. See, e.g., p. 163 and 175 ff.

88. See pp. 94 f. and p. 21 f.

89. See pp. 96 ff.

90. I.e., the Pentateuch or Torah.

91. Declaration of Principles, paragraph 2, Central Conference of American Rabbis, 1885, *The Jewish Encyclopedia* (1903 ed.), *s.v.* "Conferences, Rabbinical." Cf. pp. 21 f.

92. *Ibid.*, paragraph 4.
93. *Op. cit.*
94. *Ibid.*
95. *Ibid.*
96. *Ibid.*, paragraph 1.
97. This analysis has focused on Orthodoxy and Reform, but there are other Jewish religions that can be subjected to a similar analysis; see p. 123.
98. Exodus 19:18-20:18; Deuteronomy 5.
99. Orthodoxy claims that its covenant is the true Sinaitic covenant, but, in fact, it differs from the Sinaitic covenant as it is actually described in the Pentateuch. The Pentateuch describes a covenant between Yahveh and the Israelites whose terms require that the Israelites obey commandments that appear only in the Pentateuch. Orthodoxy maintains that the terms of the Sinaitic covenant include not only obedience by the Israelites to commandments that appear in the Pentateuch, but to those of the Talmud as well, although there is absolutely no reference to talmudic commandments in the Pentateuch or any other part of the Bible. Orthodoxy supports its view of the Sinaitic covenant by exegesis based on various hermeneutic principles that it postulates. The pentateuchal account of the Sinaitic revelation is, however, Orthodoxy's essential evidence for its covenant, so that if the Sinaitic account is false, Orthodoxy is false.
100. Louis Ginzberg sums up the matter by the flat assertion, "Judaism knows of no other than the old Sinaitic covenant"; *The Jewish Encyclopedia* (1903 ed.), *s.v.* "Covenant."
101. The ratio-moral authority principle has its ultimate justification in the revelation authority argument for a moral right to absolute authority; see pp. 16 ff.
102. I.e., such a community is either a polydox community, a latent polydox community, or a de facto polydox community; see pp. 26 ff.
103. Conservatism, owing to a variety of abrogations of talmudic law, clearly has rejected the Mosaic revelation as constituting verbal revelation. But even if the Mosaic revelation is construed as consisting only of the Pentateuch, Conservative practice reveals it has rejected the verbal status of the Mosaic revelation. Thus Conservatism permits its adherents to drive automobiles on the Sabbath. Such an action produces combustion, which is expressly prohibited on the Sabbath by the Pentateuch; Exodus 35:3. Also, the Pentateuch decrees that a menstruating woman, for approximately a period of two weeks, is in a state of impurity and makes unclean persons and things she touches; Leviticus 15:19 ff. Conservatism has generally disregarded these pentateuchal laws, but its approval of ordination for women clearly signals an overt abrogation.
104. Cf. B. Kahn, "Concepts of Authority in Conservative Judaism" (rabbinic thesis, Hebrew Union College-Jewish Institute of Religion, 1974), pp. 42-66.

105. See, e.g., Mordecai Kaplan, *Judaism as a Civilization* (New York: 1934), pp. 400 ff. Dr. Kaplan was the founder of Reconstructionism.

106. Alvin J. Reines, "Crisis, Polydoxy and Survival," *Polydoxy,* 3, No. 2/3, pp. 8 ff.

107. The Unitarian-Universalist Association is clearly an emergent religion that evolved from an historical Christianity, but there are other emergents that have not been institutionalized, as, e.g., "Death of God" Christianity.

108. A *matrix religion* may be broadly defined as the native religion out of which the founders of a new religion arise. The *emergent religion* is the new religion that these founders establish.

109. See pp. 95 ff.

Chapter V

Dialogue, Vatican II, and Contemporary Jews

The Nature of Interfaith Dialogue

In the contemporary religious world, one of the more prominent activities has been the effort at interfaith dialogue between Christians and Jews. The Second Vatican Council, as much as any other event, has been responsible for this prominence. In the "Declaration on the Relationship of the Church to Non-Christian Religions," an invitation is extended to Jews to engage in "brotherly dialogues":

> Since the spiritual patrimony common to Christians and Jews is thus so great, this sacred Synod wishes to foster and recommend that mutual understanding and respect which is the fruit above all of biblical and theological studies, and of brotherly dialogues.[1]

Vatican II not only opens the door to dialogue, it also presents a penetrating view of the nature of authentic interfaith dialogue:

> . . . "dialogue" [takes place] between competent experts from different Churches and Communities. In their meetings, which are organized in a religious spirit, each explains the teaching of his Communion in greater depth and brings out clearly its distinctive features. Through such dialogue, everyone gains a truer knowledge and more just appreciation of the teaching and religious life of both Communions.[2]

This description appears in the text with reference to the interchange that is part of the ecumenical activity intended to foster "unity among Christians."[3] Nevertheless, it accords with the dialogical spirit of Vatican II, so that we may add the word "religion" to "Communion" and thus extend this statement on dialogue to interfaith, as well as intra-Christian, communication.

One further point of great importance concerning the nature of dialogue is made in the "Decree on Ecumenism." The point is stated with reference to the Catholic position:

> The manner and order in which Catholic belief is expressed should in no way become an obstacle to dialogue with our brethren. It is, of course, essential that doctrine be clearly presented in its entirety. Nothing is so foreign to the spirit of ecumenism as a false conciliatory approach which harms the purity of Catholic doctrine and obscures its assured genuine meaning.[4]

In short, the principles governing religious dialogue, as laid down by Vatican II, are that participants present their positions to one another, that they do so in a religious spirit for the purpose of mutual understanding, and that their method be that of communicating their own positions rather than indulging in polemics against other positions. In so doing, no compromise with accuracy or authenticity is to be made; the end of dialogue is served by truth alone.

At the present stage of interfaith relations this prescription for dialogue appears to be a reasonable one. Rather than engaging in disputations over differences, the partners in dialogue should learn each other's positions and develop confidence in their ability to communicate with one another. Yet, though subscribing to these rules of dialogue in principle, problems arise when one attempts to apply them to Jewish-Catholic dialogue. There are two main difficulties, which reflect similar problems in Jewish-Christian dialogue generally. The first is that a dialogue between Catholics and Jews must inevitably become a controversy. The second is that the religious situations and religious beliefs of the majority of contemporary Jews are different from those referred to by the documents of Vatican II. We will deal with these two difficulties in order.

Dialogue Between Catholics and Jews
Must Become a Controversy

The first difficulty arises from the fact that the history and religious beliefs of Jews are considered essential elements of Catholic theology.[5] The identity of the Jews, the nature and meaning of the Bible,[6] their relation to God, their past and future, are all subjects of Catholic doctrine. There cannot, then, be a dialogue between Catholics and Jews in which Jews do not call into question and even controvert Catholic belief, for in explaining themselves and their beliefs Jews explicate a subject regarding which there already exist contrary Catholic dogmas. Yet, in dialogue, such self-explanation is precisely what Jews are called upon to give. This is no reason for Catholics and Jews to shrink from dialogue, but the problem appears clearly as we proceed to an examination of Catholic belief concerning Jews that emerged from Vatican II.

Contrary to widespread belief, the basic position of the Catholic Church regarding Jews and Jewish belief was not changed by Vatican II. The new view of the Council merely altered certain nonessential elements of the previous position. These elements were, however, most destructive, and their repudiation by Vatican II has been welcomed by enlightened religionists everywhere. As noted earlier, the beliefs of the Catholics regarding Jews and their religious views form an essential part of the Catholic religion, and we would not, therefore, expect a basic change in the nature of these beliefs unless Catholicism itself were to undergo a fundamental change. The very fact that Catholicism's beliefs regarding Jews are essential to its nature explains why, in reviewing the teaching of Vatican II respecting Jews, it is necessary to refer not only to Catholic beliefs that specifically concern Jews but to general principles of Catholic doctrine as well.

For the purposes of this review, the beliefs of Catholicism relating to Jews will be divided into three parts: the basic position on Jewish religion and history, the traditional nonessential beliefs repudiated by Vatican II, and the new beliefs prescribed by Vatican II.

Basic Catholic Position Relating To Jews

1. The Scriptures, both Old and New Testaments, are the foundation upon which the Roman Catholic religion is based and the primary source of its position regarding Jews. These Scriptures, according to the Church, were authored by God and are, therefore, inerrant and absolutely true so far as their religious content is concerned:

> Holy Mother Church, relying on the belief of the apostles, holds that the books of both the Old and New Testament in their entirety, with all their parts, are sacred and canonical because, having been written under the inspiration of the Holy Spirit they have God as their author and have been handed on as such to the Church herself. In composing the sacred books, God chose men and while employed by Him they made use of their powers and abilities, so that with Him acting in them and through them, they, as true authors, consigned to writing everything and only those things which He wanted. Therefore, since everything asserted by the inspired authors or sacred writers must be held to be asserted by the Holy Spirit, it follows that the books of Scripture must be acknowledged as teaching firmly, faithfully, and without error that truth which God wanted put into the sacred writings for the sake of our salvation.[7]

The revelation contained in the Old Testament is incomplete. Its primary purpose was to serve as a preparation for Christianity, the religion revealed in the New Testament:

> The principal purpose to which the plan of the Old Covenant was directed was to prepare for the coming both of Christ, the Universal Redeemer, and of the messianic kingdom, to announce this coming by prophecy, and to indicate its meaning through various types.[8]

The primary religious value of the Old Testament today, then, is to serve as a general support for Christianity:

> These same books [the Old Testament], then, give expression to a

lively sense of God, contain a store of sublime teachings about God, sound wisdom about human life, and a wonderful treasury of prayers, and in them the mystery of our salvation is present in a hidden way.[9]

Thus the Old Testament is fulfilled and transcended by the New Testament, but the latter will itself never be transcended; it is the final word of God:

The Christian dispensation, therefore, as the new and definitive covenant, will never pass away, and we now await no further new public revelation before the glorious manifestation of our Lord Jesus Christ.[10]

2. The concept of God revealed by Scriptures is of a person, the creator of the universe, who is omniscient, omnipotent, and self-revealing through words and miracles. God exercises providential care, intervening in history according to a divine plan for human salvation:

By an utterly free and mysterious decree of His own wisdom and goodness, the eternal Father, created the whole world. His plan was to dignify men with a participation in His own divine life. . . . He planned to assemble in the holy Church all those who would believe in Christ. Already from the beginning of the world the foreshadowing of the Church took place. She was prepared for in a remarkable way throughout the history of the people of Israel and by means of the Old Covenant. Established in the present era of time, the Church was made manifest by the outpouring of the Spirit. At the end of time she will achieve her glorious fulfillment. Then, . . . all just men from the time of Adam . . . will be gathered together with the Father in the universal Church.[11]

3. Human salvation is deliverance from sin, death, and eternal damnation. Salvation is brought about by God through Christ and the Church:

The Son, therefore, came on mission from His Father. . . . By His obedience He brought about redemption. . . . When the work which the Father had given the Son to do on earth was accomplished, the

Holy Spirit was sent on the day of Pentecost in order that He
might forever sanctify the Church, and thus all believers would
have access to the Father through Christ in the one Spirit. He is the
spirit of Life, a fountain of water springing up to life eternal.
Through Him the Father gives life to men who are dead from sin,
till at last He revives in Christ even their mortal bodies.[12]

4. The primary obstacle to salvation is original sin. This is the
sin incurred by every person as a result of Adam's disobedience against God in the Garden of Eden.[13] When Adam
violated God's commandment not to eat of the tree of knowledge, every future human being to come after him would be
conceived guilty of the sin of rebellion against God.[14] This sin
deprives humans of grace and makes them subject to evil and
death. There is no salvation without making atonement for
original sin, and there is no atonement except through baptism. The reason Jesus is indispensable for atonement is that
God's infinite majesty was offended by Adam's disobedience.
Humans, then, possessing only *finite* being, do not have the
status to atone for the *infinite* offense in which they participate through Adam. Hence no matter how profound or sin-
cere their remorse may be, humans are unable through the
use of their own powers to achieve salvation. An infinite
offense requires an infinite atonement. This atonement became available to humans with the appearance of Jesus. Jesus,
possessing divine nature (as one of the three persons of the
Godhead) and human nature (but without sin), accomplished
through his sacrifice on the cross the infinite act of atonement;
because of his divine nature he was able to do this and because of his human nature the sacrifice came from the of-
fenders.[15] Thus the primary obstacle to salvation, original sin,
is removed.

5. Since God, in his infinite mercy, wished mankind to attain
salvation, it was necessary to bring them to Jesus Christ, the
only possible means of salvation. It is here that Jews play
their role in the cosmic drama. God, beginning with Abraham, chose the Jews as the ones who would prepare the
world for the coming of Jesus. Accordingly, He revealed to

the Jews such knowledge of Himself as was appropriate in a world without Christ,[16] and communicated to them His promise of future salvation for all humankind.

In this way the world would be prepared to recognize Jesus as the Christ when he came to fulfill that promise:

> In carefully planning and preparing the salvation of the whole human race, the God of supreme love, by a special dispensation, chose for Himself a people to whom He might entrust His promises. First He entered into a covenant with Abraham and, through Moses, with the people of Israel. To this people which He had acquired for Himself, He so manifested Himself through words and deeds as the one true and living God that Israel came to know by experience the ways of God with men, and with God Himself speaking to them through the mouth of the prophets, Israel daily gained a deeper and clearer understanding of His ways and made them more widely known among the nations. The plan of salvation, foretold by the sacred authors, recounted and explained by them, is found as the true word of God in the books of the Old Testament: these books, therefore, written under divine inspiration, remain permanently valuable. . . . Now the books of the Old Testament, in accordance with the state of mankind before the time of salvation established by Christ, reveal to all men the knowledge of God and of man and the ways in which God, just and merciful, deals with men. These books, though they also contain some things which are incomplete and temporary, nevertheless show us true divine pedagogy.[17]

6. Once Jesus appeared, the preparatory phase of God's plan for human salvation ended. There was no further mission, task, or need for biblical Judaism. Before the advent of Jesus, the nearest man could come to God was through biblical Judaism;[18] Jesus having come, it became a fossil. It was no longer the true religion; and Jews were no longer the Chosen People. The new People of God were the Christians; to be saved Jews must convert to Christianity.

> He [God] . . . chose the race of Israel as a people unto Himself. With it He set up a covenant. Step by step He taught this people by manifesting in its history both Himself and the decree of His will,

and by making it holy unto Himself. All these things, however, were done by way of preparation and as a figure of that new and perfect covenant which was to be ratified in Christ, and of that more luminous revelation which was to be given through God's very Word made flesh.

"Behold the days shall come, saith the Lord, and I will make a new covenant with the house of Israel,[19] and with the house of Judah. . . .I will be their God, and they shall be my people. . . . For all shall know me, from the least of them even to the greatest, saith the Lord" (Jer. 31:1-34). Christ instituted this new covenant, that is to say, the new testament, in His blood. . . . This was to be the new People of God. For, those who believe in Christ, who are reborn not from a perishable but from an imperishable seed through the Word of the living God, not from the flesh but from water and the Holy Spirit, are finally established as "a chosen race, a royal priesthood, a holy nation. . . ."[20]

7. Yet the Jews did not accept Christianity. Although they were the people chosen to receive God's promise of the coming Messiah, they did not recognize or acknowledge Jesus as the Messiah.

8. At this point, Vatican II prescribes new doctrine to replace the traditional beliefs. The traditional beliefs may be described as follows:

   a. The Jews not only refused to accept Christianity and acknowledge Jesus as the Christ, they repudiated him. They charged he was a false Messiah; they brought about his arrest; they insisted upon his execution; and they were satisfied with his crucifixion. The Jews did this as an entire people, willfully and maliciously. They should have known better, since their own Scriptures had foretold the coming of Jesus as the Christ.

   b. The entire Jewish people till the end of time is guilty of this crime.[21] They were and are unrepentant deicides. For their crime, the following divine punishments have been decreed by God against the Jews: they are now the Accursed rather than the Chosen People; they are now a purblind race, spiritually deadened and unable to see the truth of Christianity; their religion is now invalid, if anything, an obstacle to the true religion; they are to be dispersed over the face of the earth and undergo various persecutions until the end of history when they will be converted to Christianity as a group. The continuing dispersion and suffering of the Jews may be taken as a sign of the justice of God and the truth of Catholicism.[22] A legitimate conclusion from this view is that persecution of the Jews is a good thing. For example, we find the following decrees (among others) enacted by the Fathers of the Fourth Lateran Council:

> Jews may not appear in public during Easter week; Jews must give tithes on their houses and other property to the Church and pay a yearly tax at Easter; no Christian prince may give an office to a Jew under pain of excommunication; Jews must wear a distinctive dress from their twelfth year to distinguish them from Christians.[23]

9. Vatican II instituted the following changes in paragraphs 8a and 8b above:

a. While the Jews do not accept Jesus as the Christ, still they are esteemed by God:

> As holy Scripture testified, Jerusalem did not recognize the time of her visitation, nor did the Jews in large number accept the gospel; indeed, not a few opposed the spreading of it. Nevertheless, according to the Apostle, the Jews still remain most dear to God because of their fathers,[24] for He does not repent of the gifts He makes nor of the calls He issues.[25]

b. While certain Jews did urge the death of Christ, not all Jews are guilty of this crime:

> True, authorities of the Jews and those who followed their lead pressed for the death of Christ; still, what happened in His passion cannot be blamed upon all the Jews then living, without distinction, nor upon the Jews of today.[26]

c. While the Jews are no longer God's Chosen People, neither are they the Accursed People:

> Although the Church is the new people of God, the Jews should not be presented as repudiated or cursed by God, as if such views followed from the holy Scriptures.[27]

d. While Judaism is no longer a true religion, the religion of the Old Testament still retains a certain degree of historical, pedagogical, and sentimental value:

> For the Church of Christ acknowledges that, according to the mystery of God's saving design, the beginnings of her faith and her election are already found among the patriarchs, Moses, and the prophets . . . . The Church, therefore, cannot forget that she received the revelation of the Old Testament through the people with whom God in his inexpressible mercy deigned to establish the Ancient Covenant. Nor can she forget that she draws sustenance from the root of that good olive tree onto which have been grafted the wild olive branches of the Gentiles. . . . The Church recalls too that from the Jewish people sprang the apostles, her foundation stones and pillars, as well as most of the early disciples who proclaimed Christ to the world.[28]

e. As a consequence of the above beliefs, persecution of the Jews is repudiated; and in the fullness of time, the Jews will all be converted to Christianity.

> The Church repudiates all persecutions against any man. Moreover, mindful of her common patrimony with the Jews, and motivated by the gospel's spiritual love and by no political considerations, she deplores the hatred, persecutions, and displays of anti-Semitism directed against the Jews at any time and from any source.[29]
>
> In company with the prophets and the same Apostle, the Church awaits that day, known to God alone, on which all peoples will address the Lord in a single voice and "serve him with one accord."[30]

As is apparent, the Second Vatican Council has removed certain pernicious and nonessential beliefs concerning the Jews from traditional Catholic doctrine. Still the Council has left intact the basic Catholic position: that Jews were involved in the crucifixion of Jesus, one of the persons of the Godhead;[31] that Judaism, having been superseded by Christianity, the only true religion, is no longer a saving religion; and that the conversion of the Jews to Catholicism, which is presently awaited and hoped for, will be accomplished in the Messianic Age.

In themselves, these beliefs are not socially objectionable:[32] a monopoly on truth and salvation is the claim of virtually every orthodox revealed religion.[33] True, such beliefs among Catholics have often led in the past to such objectionable conclusions as "All Jews are guilty of deicide," and "God has granted the Church the right to harrass and persecute the Jews." These conclusions have now been disavowed by Vatican II. When carefully followed and scrupulously taught, it may be hoped that these beliefs, as presented by Vatican II, will not foster anti-Semitism.

Why the Basic Catholic Position on Jews Leads to Controversy

Still, the preceding review of Roman Catholic belief regarding Jews demonstrates the first difficulty of dialogue between Catholics and Jews stated above, namely, that a dialogue between Catholics and Jews must inevitably lead to controversy. Jews must deny the truth of Catholic teaching regarding the nature of the Bible, Jewish belief, Jesus, and Jesus' death; for if this teaching is not denied, Jews cannot maintain that their own beliefs are valid. In other words, if Catholic teaching regarding the Bible, Jewish belief, Jesus, and Jesus' death are true, then no Jewish religious system can be true. This is seen clearly in the following summary of three basic points of difference.

Catholicism maintains that the purpose of the Bible (or Old Testament) was to present a religion or old covenant whose function was to serve as preparation for the religion or new covenant of the New Testament with its central belief that Jesus is the Christ. Although Jews may disagree with one another over the nature of the Bible, all would deny that it contains any awareness of or reference to Jesus, let alone foreshadows his future coming as the Messiah.

Catholicism also asserts that the New Testament is inerrant and eternal truth, a revelation that has fulfilled and transcended the Bible but which itself will never be transcended. Jews, of course, must reject this assertion, for accepting it is equivalent to accepting the truth of Catholicism or some other Christianity. The consensus among Jews is that the New Testament is not supernatural revelation at all, but a fallible document written by humans.

Lastly, since the only objective evidence offered that Jesus is the Christ is the New Testament, and for Jews the New Testament is a human, fallible document, there exists no credible evidence for Jews that Jesus is the Christ and part of the Godhead, and this notion is, therefore, rejected. Moreover, inasmuch as Jesus is not believed to be part of the Godhead, if there were Jews involved in the death of Jesus, however wrong their actions may have been, they were not deicides.

Vatican II Misrepresents Contemporary Jewish Religious Situation and Religious Beliefs

We come then to the second difficulty present in Catholic-Jewish dialogue: the religious situation and beliefs of contemporary Jews contradict the way they are depicted by the documents of Vatican II. There are two facets of the Vatican II misconception. The first is that contemporary Jews all adhere to one religion, which may be referred to as Old Testament Biblicism.[34] The second is that Jews share many basic religious concepts with the Catholics, including theistic absolutism; that the Bible (Old Testament) is literal, infallible revelation; and the coming of a Messiah.

The View That All Jews Adhere to the Same Religion Is a Misconception

As pointed out in an earlier discussion, the view that all Jews adhere to one religion is a widespread misconception.[35] That Jews adhere to different religious systems is readily apparent by the fact there are at least five formally distinct Jewish religious organizational structures: Orthodox; Conservative; Reform; Reconstructionist; and Polydox. Moreover, adding to the complexity, the latter four organizations are themselves not monolithic, but encompass a spectrum of religious ideas. Many Conservative Jews subscribe virtually to the Orthodox position, others come very near to Reform; some Reform Jews agree closely with the naturalism of Reconstructionism, others favor neo-orthodoxy. Many members of the non-orthodox Judaisms agree with the freedom of Polydoxy. It is not possible here to enter in detail upon all the rich variety that these organizations produce and embrace. Still, it is helpful to illustrate at least in part the actual situation of the different religions referred to loosely by the name "Judaism" so that Catholic dialogists (and Christian dialogists generally) may be helped to understand their many partners in dialogue. We can take for this purpose the various theological positions widely held today among Jews, and divide them into two broad categories. These will be termed the traditional and modernist positions. The former is held by Orthodox and many Conservative Jews, the latter is taken mainly by Reform, Reconstructionist, and Polydox Jews.

The Traditional Jewish Position

The foundation of true religion in the traditional position is God's revelation to Moses. This revelation, the Torah, consists of two parts, the Pentateuch or Written Law, and the Talmud or Oral Law. God authored every word of the Torah, which is on this account literally and infallibly true. The Torah expresses God's will for man, and obedience to the Torah brings salvation. In addition to the Torah, there have been supplementary revelations; these are contained in the Prophets and Hagiographa. There has not, however, ever been nor will there ever be a revelation that supersedes or alters the Torah; the perfect God does not change and revoke the words expressing his divine will and omniscience.

The Modernist Jewish Position

The modernist position does not easily lend itself to generalization. Nevertheless, virtually all modernists hold certain principles in common which may be summarized as follows:

1. The foundation of modernism can be described as a negation, the denial that the Bible is a literal and infallible revelation from a theistic God. Some modernists consider the Bible partially revealed or inspired, others think it entirely the work of humans. Whichever position is adhered to, modernists explicitly or implicitly agree that the Bible is fallible and individuals must decide for themselves what is true in Scriptures.[36] Thus modernists take upon themselves personal decision-making as part of their religious responsibility. The narratives of the Pentateuch that describe an oracular and miracle-working deity are generally regarded as mythological. There is substantial accord, however, regarding the value of the ethical teachings of the prophets, particularly of such preexilic prophets as Amos and First Isaiah. Although the Pentateuch is understood to be largely mythological, both it and other historical religious works serve as sources of ritual, symbolism, and liturgical language. Modernism can be viewed as continuing the biblical and traditional quest of Jews for religious authenticity.
2. The religious systems to which modernist Jews subscribe are open to change. For this reason they do not feel the modernist position need ever be superseded, not because significantly new religious ideas never arise, but because open religious systems can embrace and absorb them as they do.
3. There is no one view of deity subscribed to in modernist Judaism. Nontheistic as well as theistic theologies are advanced. Such concepts as the finite God (personal and impersonal), pantheism, and panentheism find favor. A number of modernists are also greatly influenced by naturalism and empiricism. While the specifics of modernist theologies differ, at times greatly, some theological generalizations relevant to our theme may be drawn from modernist thought. Divine providence is generally not sought in miraculous intervention by a deity into

human affairs, but in the "ordinary" or "natural" potentialities for good that are available for realization by human effort. Also, no one group is seen as chosen by a deity for a special task or for special favor and love. All who do the good are "chosen people." The concept of the "Chosen People" as it appears in Scripture is by and large regarded as mythological.

4. The concept of salvation, that is, soteria, also varies in modernist Judaism. Resurrection is universally rejected by modernists, although a number affirm the immortality of the soul. Many modernists, however, in agreement with pentateuchal and prophetic Jewish systems, reject the notion that there is a religiously significant afterlife. Soteria is a state of meaningfulness that is to be found and enjoyed in this life. The primary obstacle to soteria is generally viewed not as sin, but as the finite condition of humans which makes their existence subject to angst and death.[37]

5. Modernists, generally, hope and work for a stage of human history that is termed by some the Messianic Age. But the concept of a supernatural and miraculous end to ordinary history through the agency of a human or divine Messiah is rejected by the modernist. The Messianic Age, a time of universal goodwill, justice, and material plenty, will be ushered in by the realization of the human potential for goodness.

Vatican II Presumes Traditional Judaism, with Which It Shares General Fundamental Principles, to Be the Religion of All Jews

Upon examining the traditional and modernist Jewish positions, it is evident the documents of Vatican II take traditional Judaism to be the religion of all Jews. Catholicism can, understandably, find itself quite comfortable with this traditional position, for the fundamental agreement on the nature and general principles of religion between Catholicism and traditional Judaism is clear.[38] The foundations of religion for both are literal, infallible revelations from a theistic God; both accept the Bible (or Old Testament) as literal, infallible revelation; each affirms salvation as consisting of a blessed, personal afterlife; and each asserts the belief that ordinary history will come to an end with the supernatural advent of a Messiah. The differences consist in details of belief.[39] Traditional Judaism maintains the revelation in the Bible (or Old Testament) is true forever; Catholicism claims it has been superseded by the New Testament revelation, which, in turn, is asserted to be true forever. Traditional Judaism maintains the theistic Godhead consists of one person; Catholicism teaches the theistic Godhead consists of three persons. Traditional Judaism believes salvation and eternal life are attained by obedience to the commandments of the Bible (or Old Testament) and Talmud;[40] Catholicism says salvation and eternal life can only come through the acceptance of the New Testament and Jesus as the Christ. Traditional Judaism says the Messiah will come but has not yet come; Catholicism contends he has come and will come again.

These details are the differences that have historically been understood to constitute the distinction between Orthodox Judaism and Catholicism, as can be seen when the issues that occupied the Jews and Catholics in the great disputations of the Middle Ages are examined. At the famous disputation in 1263 at Barcelona, between Nahmanides and Pablo Christiani, the issues in question were whether the Messiah had yet appeared, and whether the Messiah according to Scripture is a divine or human being.[41] At Tortosa in 1413-14, a disputation held at the command of the antipope Benedict XIII (Pedro de Luna), the issue was whether Jesus could be proved the Messiah on the basis of the Talmud.[42] It seems reasonable to conclude that Vatican II envisaged that the dialogue it proposed between Jews and Catholics would take a form substantively similar to that of the medieval disputation. The two groups being in general agreement on the basic nature of religion, namely, belief in a theistic deity, infallible revelation, supernatural salvation, a Messiah, and an afterlife, would then discuss their differences over details. But if the primary differences between traditional Judaism and Catholicism can be adequately discussed in a medieval-style disputation over differences in details, such is not the case with respect to the differences beween modernist Judaism and Catholicism. Here the differences are deep and fundamental, reflecting the profound cleavage between religion such as modernist Judaism represents, whose roots are in the modern age, and religion such as Catholicism, whose roots are in antiquity and the Middle Ages.

Fundamental Differences Exist Between
Catholicism and Modernist Judaism

A summary of some fundamental differences between modernist Judaism and Catholicism quickly reveals the depth of disagreement between them. Catholicism maintains the Bible is an infallible revelation from a theistic God; modernist Judaism states the Bible is a fallible document, and that no literal, infallible revelation from a theistic God exists. Catholicism believes that its hierarchy and teachings possess authority over its adherents and the latter must obey them; in modernist Judaism the individual adherent exercises self-authority. Catholicism sees itself as possessing the final revelation and ultimate religious truth; modernist Judasim regards itself as open to new religious truth when and if it arises. Catholicism regards theism as essential to religion, modernist Judaism includes both theistic and nontheistic views of reality. Finally, central to Catholicism is belief in a supernatural Messiah, Jesus, who has come once and will come again; in modernist Judaism the very concept of a supernatural Messiah is rejected.

Dialogue Remains Possible Between Catholics and Jews

Clearly enough, dialogue between Catholics and modernist Jews presents a far greater challenge than that between Catholics and traditional Jews. The reason is evident from the preceding: modernist Jews reject the concepts that establish the very foundations of Catholicism, concepts that traditional Judaism affirms.

Yet despite the increased complexity the above exposition reveals is present in any realistic dialogue between Catholics and Jews, the avowed aims of dialogue are in no way stultified.[43]

These aims are understanding and regard for each other's existence. Genuine understanding and regard cannot arise except through authentic communication, and the latter takes place only in a meeting between those who see and accept one another in their concrete actuality. Dialogue, in a sense, is easier for the modernist than for the Orthodox or Catholic religionist. By the very fact that modernists do not possess absolute truth, they find themselves open to the claims of truth made by others; it is less natural to give a hearing to other viewpoints when one believes oneself to be in possession of ultimate and final knowledge. There can be little question that profound and fundamental differences of belief exist between Jews, particulary modernists, and Catholics. Still, the ethical base of the call for dialogue points to a great and transcending truth. It is not necessary for persons to believe together in order to live together, as it is not necessary for them to affirm the truth of one another's beliefs in order to affirm the value of one another's existence.

Notes

1. The Documents of Vatican II, ed. W. M. Abbott, S. J. (N.Y.: The America Press, 1966), p. 665. In a note (21) to this statement, the translator makes the point even more explicit. "The Declaration endorses and promotes dialogue between Christians and Jews, just as the Decree on Ecumenism endorses and promotes dialogue between the separated Christian groups." (The *Documents of Vatican II* will hereafter be designated by *DV II*.)
2. *DV II*, p. 347.
3. *Ibid.*
4. *DV II*, p. 354.
5. The converse is not true. Christianity plays no essential role in Jewish religious systems. The religion of a group such as the "Jews for Jesus" is not regarded as a Jewish religious system.
6. I.e., the Old Testament. Jews do not use the designation "Old Testament" since they do not accept the existence of a new one. The term Old Testament is retained where confusion would result otherwise.
7. *DV II*, pp. 118 f.
8. *DV II*, p. 122.
9. *Ibid.*
10. *Ibid.*, p. 113. It is of interest to note that Muslims maintain the New Testament was superseded by the Koran.

11. *Ibid.*, pp. 15 f.

12. *Ibid.*, pp. 16 f.

13. *Ibid.*, p. 15; *et al.*

14. Except the Virgin Mary, by virtue of the Immaculate Conception.

15. According to the Christology defined at the Ecumenical Council of Chalcedon in 451 and accepted by all major Christian bodies (including the Roman Catholic Church), the two natures, divine and human, exist in Jesus Christ *without confusion, without change, without division, and without separation* (Enchiridion Symbolorum, Definitionum et Declarationum de Rebus Fidei et Morum, 36th ed., edited by H. Denziger and A. Schönmetzer [Rome: Herder, 1976], no. 302). This is a paradox and is recognized as such by the churches (it is often referred to as the "divine" or "holy paradox").

For the different Christian views concerning atonement, see Gustav Aulén, *Den kristna försoningstanken* (1930); abridged English version, *Christus Victor* (1931).

16. I.e., only partial or incomplete truth could be given. This explains for Catholics why there are no explicit references to Jesus in the Old Testament. Jews, of course, maintain there are no references at all to Jesus in the Bible (Old Testament), neither explicit nor implicit.

17. *DV II*, pp. 121 f.

18. Before Christ biblical Judaism did not offer salvation. Only Christianity can do that. Before Christ, however, biblical Judaism was the "nearest" humans could come to God.

19. Jewish and critical Bible scholars generally maintain this "new covenant" has nothing to do with Christianity. It refers rather to a new covenant, as it says, with the House of Israel or the Jews, i.e., an internal reform of biblical Judaism. These are the differences of interpretation between Catholics and Jews that are taken up in dialogue.

20. *DV II*, p. 25.

21. This is in addition, of course, to their continuing unexpiated guilt resulting from the original sin.

22. The state of Israel presented a problem to some Catholics because of this view. To reconcile the state of Israel with their beliefs they held it would be short-lived.

23. *DV II*, p. 667, n. 28.

24. That is, not because of any merit on the part of the Jews today. They reject Jesus, whereas the Catholic believe Abraham, Moses, etc., did not.

25. *DV II*, p. 664.

26. *Ibid.*, pp. 665 f.

27. *Ibid.*, p. 666.

28. *Ibid.*, p. 664.

29. *Ibid.*, pp. 666 f.

30. *Ibid.*, pp. 664 f. A note (19) to this passage reads, "A reference to the 'conversion' of the Jews was removed from an earlier version of this

Declaration, because many Council Fathers felt it was not appropriate in a document striving to establish common goals and interest first."

31. Those Jews from the point of view of Catholicism, even after Vatican II, are still considered deicides; see *DV II,* p. 666, n. 23. No Jew, of course, believes this proposition is true. There are Jews who, on the basis of the New Testament, believe that some Jews were involved in Jesus' death (critically speaking, the evidence is not conclusive, and opinions among Jews, as among modern Christians, vary). However, Jews do not believe that God has the form or nature of a human, or that Jesus was or is part of the Godhead.

32. I.e., objectionable on the grounds that they lead, unnecessarily and unreasonably, to deteriorated social relations. They remain "religiously objectionable" to those who consider them false, and members of other religions do.

33. E.g., Orthodox Judaism and Sunni Islam.

34. Cf. p. 79.

35. See pp. 79 ff.

36. Hence, moderninsts are avowed polydoxians or latent and de facto polydoxians.

37. See pp. 59 ff.

38. Both subscribe, for example, to a definition of religion that can be described as "belief in theistic absolutism"; see p. 56.

39. These are details from the viewpoint of philosophy of religion in its general classification of religions. To the religionists involved these details may, quite properly, be considered essential and saving differences.

40. The Talmud, as well as the Pentateuch, is believed by traditional Judaism to have been revealed to Moses.

41. Traditional Judaism believes the Messiah is only human; Catholics, of course, believe he is divine, part of the Godhead. There was a sad aftermath to this disputation. Nahmanides was forced into exile to flee the wrath of the Dominicans. Disputations, together with the coercion, fear, and persecution that often accompanied them, are now repudiated by Vatican II. Dialogue, with its spirit of respect, replaces the disputation.

42. The Talmud, which makes some disparaging remarks about non-Jewish religions, was often attacked in the Middle Ages. These remarks were not doctrinal, but simply asides. Nevertheless, the Talmud was often condemned. For example, after the disputation at Tortosa, study of the Talmud was prohibited. Often it was consigned to the flames. The issue of the Talmud is still alive for some Catholics. We read the following comment to the text of the Declaration concerning the Jews, "Cardinal Ruffini, Archbishop of Palermo, (requested) that Christians should love Jews, and Jews should declare they will not hate Christians (and he asked that certain passages in the Talmud be corrected)." *DV II,* p. 665, n. 20.

43. In general, the remarks made here with reference to dialogue between Jews and Catholics holds for dialogue between Jews and Protestants, especially fundamentalist Protestants.

Chapter VI

God and Polydox Theology

Polydoxy is a form of religion that affirms the ultimate right of the individual to religious autonomy. There are, however, semantic impediments that can inhibit the exercise of this freedom. This inhibition is to a significant degree induced by the conditioning of persons in our culture to think that certain terms have and can only have one legitimate meaning, when, in fact, such terms may have a number of legitimate meanings, and can even properly acquire new meanings. Two terms whose free use is fundamental for the exercise of individual religious autonomy are *theology* and *God.* In this chapter, these terms will be taken up and provided with meanings appropriate for a polydoxy. In addition, to demonstrate concretely their compatibility with a particular polydox system, these meanings will be placed into a context of a Polydox Jewish theology.[1] It should be borne in mind, however, that what is true of a Polydox Jewish theology holds in principle for all polydox systems.[2]

At first blush, the most prominent feature of the terms theology, God, and Jewish is that none of them possesses a univocal meaning. The term theology is taken from Greek philosophy, and was used by neither Jews nor Christians until late in their history.[3] The term God, derived from the Gothic *guth,* has been used by philosophers as well as religionists in a bewildering variety of senses. The very word Jew, from which the terms Jewish as well as Judaism derive, came into existence long after the age of the biblical Hebrews and Israelites.[4] Hence our subject can be pursued from the point of view of historical philology, in which the many uses of the past are defined and catalogued but which in no way lays down authoritative univocal meanings. The concern here, however, is not with the past, but with advancing selected and even new meanings for polydox use.

The Legitimate Use of Religious Language

It will be useful before entering upon our subject proper to discuss a problem that arises in a polydoxy, but which also has occurred often in the history of religious philosophy. This is a problem of communication that concerns the legitimate use of religious language. In the course of the present exposition, new meanings for old terms will be introduced. It is the fashion in some theological circles to disguise such creative activity and pretend that the new meaning is that which the term has always signified. In the Middle Ages, fear of persecution and a lack of critical scholarship combined to justify such deception. This justification no longer exists. The practice of deception, conscious or unconscious, is as debasing to theology as it is destructive to scientific scholarship. No pretense of continuous meaning, therefore, will be made where none exists. Theology is not, after all, the sly rebuttal of science.

The question may then be raised whether it is proper to employ a term in a novel manner, so that no direct historical justification for the usage can be given. The immediate and fundamental answer to this question is that words belong to those who use them. This principle has been applied on countless occasions in intellectual and religious history, whenever a generation has given names to its new perspectives and insights in the language bequeathed to it by its predecessors. The consensus of society is that this principle is proper and sound; and that inquiry into a new meaning is therefore eminently more profitable than condemnation of those who have strayed from an old one. Thus it is scholarship to explore the attributes of Yahveh according to the Pharisees or Maimonides, and idle cavil to censure them for having altered the connotation decreed by Amos. Words, then, as modern lexicography now universally admits, have no one legitimate or authoritative meaning; and their use with new meanings is a process apparently destined to continue so long as humans, knowledge, and society continue to advance and evolve.[5]

However, there is perhaps a nuance to our question which the answer above does not resolve. This is the implication that there is an element of conscious deception in employing religious language in a novel sense. Whereas it is granted that the words of the general culture possess no one legitimate meaning, it seems to be argued that the words of religion do, or at the least that they have meanings which are approved. The objection may be stated this way: Certain words have signified specific beliefs of which the audience approves; the audience expects someone who employs these words to mean these beliefs; if the user does not mean these beliefs, he is deceiving the audience into thinking that he holds these beliefs in order to avoid their disapproval and its consequences.

We will give two answers to this objection. First, in many cases it is based on the false premise that such terms as "God," "Jewish," and "theology" are univocal, and possess, therefore, a single meaning. They do not; many different meanings of these terms have existed historically and continue to exist. Second, and more important, we have here an instance of what may be called the *fallacy of orthodox expectation*. The primary basis of this objection is a belief in orthodoxy and dogmas, and the objection fully stated takes this form: there are certain obligatory beliefs or dogmas; certain words have signified these dogmas; and the fact that one does not accept these dogmas is furtively disguised by employing in a new sense the words that have in the past signified these dogmas. The answer to this objection is given by the philosophy of polydoxy: in a polydoxy there are no dogmas of this kind. Accordingly, persons who come to a polydoxy with the expectation of dogmatic definition labor under a misconception: the fallacy of orthodox expectation in a polydox religious situation.

Communication Legitimatizes the Use of Language

The only valid basis on which an objection can be raised in a polydoxy against the use of terms with new meanings is the practical one of communication. Does it better serve the purpose of communication in a polydoxy to invent new terms, or is there an economy effected in retaining the old where possible? The answer, in the author's view, is that it is more efficient where possible to retain the old terms. Among the reasons:

1. These terms invariably possess more than one historical meaning at the present, and none, therefore, can be employed in a systematic work, even to connote a past sense, without defining which sense of the past is meant. Consequently, since definition is required in any case, what does it matter whether the definition is drawn from previous usage or is a new one?
2. A new meaning is not entirely unrelated to the old one in that it is intended to replace it. Laying down a new definition, then, implies one of two things regarding the old meaning: that it is incorrect, or, if not necessarily incorrect, that it is inadequate for the purposes of a polydoxy. In either case, appropriation of the same name for the new meaning signifies that the old meaning has been considered and rejected as unsuitable.
3. Words have uses other than as signs conveying references. Among such uses are the expression and evocation of attitudes. Hence the word God, for example, apart from its capacity to refer to a reality, has the power as well to direct a positive attitude toward this reality. Some, who entirely deny a reality reference to the term God, argue for its retention on the basis of its power to evoke human feelings.[6] Spinoza, although he rejects theism, nonetheless gives the name God to substance in the belief that it is the proper object of certain positive attitudes that the word God evokes. Likewise, in our retaining the word theology, although a new meaning for the term will be suggested, a positive attitude is expressed toward

the new activity designated. This use of words for other than intellectual communication is deeply ingrained in the actuality of the word itself. And unlike intellectual meanings, this kind of communication is transferred to other words only with the greatest difficulty. Investigation into the nonintellectual uses of language provides a large chapter in the work of contemporary philosophy. Suffice it to say that these uses are particularly important in the case of religion, where it is the entire psyche of humans that is the object of concern, and not the communication of intellectual meaning alone.

Theology

Having said this, let us return to our subject proper. The first word to engage us is *theology*. This word as such possesses no significant or clear history of religious usage. Perhaps this is the reason in part that its use today communicates such varied and even contradictory meanings. It should be noted, however, that almost from its inception in Aristotle, theology has been employed by religionists and philosophers to represent many meanings, so that usage today in religion and philosophy shows a similar salmagundi. The many uses of the word theology as stated above do not concern us, except to note that the word is a general problem. Our interest is in arriving at a meaning suitable to a polydoxy. We will, therefore, limit ourselves to the following points: the basic or classical definition of theology; a definition appropriate to a polydoxy; and an analysis of the major forms theology has taken, including the forms that are consistent with a polydoxy.

The Classical and Polydox Definitions of Theology

The classical definition of theology is "the science or study that treats of God, his nature and attributes, and his relations to humankind and the universe." This definition, it will be argued presently, is not entirely suited to polydox use. Still, one can agree with its limitation of the term theology to the study of God. This excludes the confusing use of theology to refer to the study of religious experience in general.

Yet the classical definition of theology is still not appropriate to a polydoxy. Appropriateness is here determined by a twofold rule: 1) no part of a religion, such as its theology, can be inconsistent with the essence of the religion; 2) where a part of a religion admits of two or more definitions consistent with the religion's essence, the definition most coherent with the essence is to be preferred. A polydox community has been described as one in which members of the community are affirmed in their autonomy, and that, consequently, all opinions of polydoxians on such subjects as God are equally valid so far as the polydox institution is concerned. In the classical definition, the statement that theology is "the science or study that treats of God, his nature, and attributes," the assumption is clearly present that there exists an *ens reale* (real being) into which theology inquires. Theology in a polydoxy, however, particularly one respectful of scientific method, cannot proceed in this uncritical and dogmatic manner. There are those in a polydoxy who out of their freedom may choose to deny a reality reference to the term God, yet whose study in arriving at this conclusion is their theology or inquiry into "God." A definition of theology appropriate to a polydoxy should then include their activity. Moreover, the name theology applied to their inquiry is proper in that it communicates the nuance of approval for the activity it designates, that the study of "God" pursued by these persons has the same institutional imprimatur in a polydoxy as the study of those whose conclusions are more congenial with those of historical theological activity. Accordingly, a definition of theology that may be offered as coherent with the essence of a polydoxy is the following: *Theology is the science or study that treats of the meaning of the word God.*

This definition satisfies both polydox and scientific needs: the former, in that polydoxians who study the possible views that can be held regarding the word God engage in "theology" whatever their conclusions about these views may be; the latter, inasmuch as polydoxians who theologize are not committed beforehand to any particular conclusion, and can, therefore, pursue their investigation in a critical and scientific manner without presuppositions. Furthermore, this definition requires no significant change in the classical use of the term theology, since it continues to include all the activity the term in the past has denoted. Its usage is merely extended to cover all the activity of the present age. This definition makes of theology an unrestricted ongoing enterprise, with the capacity to serve a community that can accept the view that knowledge and religion are continuously open to change.

Forms of Theology

By the forms of theology are meant those general procedures that have been followed in establishing a meaning for the word God. We will concern ourselves with those forms that serve to establish the meaning of the word God as reference to a real existent. These forms may be classified as follows:

1. Theology that is based on an authoritative revelation. An authoritative revelation is one that a religious community accepts as possessing an absolute right to dictate the community's beliefs. This form of theology is the primary means of establishing a reality referent of God in such religions as Orthodox Judaism, Roman Catholicism, and fundamentalist Protestantism. Since the adherents of these religions accept either the Bible, or the Bible and New Testament, as authoritative, the reality they accept as God is established for them by showing that these writings affirm such a reality. This form of theology is inappropriate for a polydoxy since it is inconsistent with the principle of polydox philosophy that there exists no authoritative revelation so far as the polydox community as a whole is concerned. Thus there exists no authoritative body of knowledge or belief whose affirmation

is obligatory upon the members of a polydox community.

2. Theology that is based on certain and irrefragable natural knowledge. Examples of theologies that claim to proceed in this manner are Aristotle's *Metaphysics* and Spinoza's *Ethics*. If such a theology were to be demonstrated it would, of course, compel assent and be rationally authoritative. No present claim, however, to such knowledge has been convincingly demonstrated.

3. Theology that is based on both infallible authoritative revelation and certain natural knowledge, and which seeks to reconcile whatever conflicts or contradictions appear to exist between them. Saadiah, among the Jews, and Thomas Aquinas, among the Christians, are representative exponents of this mode of theologizing, which was prevalent throughout the Middle Ages. Theology of this form is inappropriate to a polydoxy for the reasons given in evaluating forms one and two above.

4. Theology that is based on subjective evidence.[7] This evidence is subjective—so far as the religious community as a whole is concerned—because the experience occurs privately to one or several members of the community and is not or cannot be shared or verified by the other members. Reported examples of such experience are: prophetic visions; apprehension of a presence or power taken to be God; mystic union; private witnessing of a miracle; and other experiences, as, for example, the I-Thou relation Martin Buber describes. This form of theology is consistent with a polydoxy. It should be borne in mind, however, that the evaluation of theological evidence as subjective has as its corollary the judgment that the theology has no authority. There is no sensible reason why the members of a religious community should accept the beliefs of a fellow-religionist on the latter's unverifiable assertion that there exists private evidence for those beliefs. History is replete with false messiahs and the tragic consequences of authority exercised in the name of subjective theology. Hence such a theology is consistent with a polydoxy only when a re-

nunciation of authority is understood to accompany it.

5. Theology that is based on objective evidence.[9] The basic characteristics of objective evidence are that it is apprehended publicly and by natural human faculties. Generally stated, evidence is objective for a community of religionists if, all necessary natural conditions having been met, every member of the community can experience it. Since new members are continually entering a community, objective experience must be repeatable at will. Experiences that are unique, as for example, the reported cleavage of the Red Sea, are objective only to the persons who witness them. Since such events cannot be produced at will, the testimony of those who witness them is subjective evidence to those who have not observed the event directly. Theology based upon the evidence of objective repeatable experience, like all natural knowledge critically considered, is fallible and therefore probable. Since such theology is open to error, it is not authoritative so far as a religious community as a whole is concerned, and is, therefore, suitable for a polydoxy. Methods of determining truth such as pragmatism, coherence, and empirical verifiability are employed in this form of theology.

Jewish

The word we next turn to is *Jewish*.[10] What meaning does the word have in the phrase Polydox Jewish theology? At first thought, it would seem that a theology properly called Jewish would be identical with theology that has been called Jewish in the past. We may term this the static use of the term Jewish, and the criterion of identity with the past, the *static rule*. The simplicity of the static rule is obvious and appealing. Unhappily, the static use of the term Jewish is impossible as regards Polydox Jewish theology. For at least three reasons, each of which is decisive by itself, the static rule cannot be applied to give meaning to the term Jewish in the phrase "Polydox Jewish theology."[11] The first is factual, the second essential, the third practical.

First, Polydox Judaism, by denying literal and infallible revelation, breaks with the Jewish religious systems that originated prior to the nineteenth century. Hence if the static rule were to be followed, there could be no Polydox Judaism, and consequently, no Polydox Jewish theology at all. Thus Polydox Judaism, by the very fact of its existence, repudiates the static rule.[12]

Second, any meaning of the word Jewish appropriate to Polydox Judaism must be appropriate to the essence of a polydoxy, which renounces authoritative and obligatory theological beliefs or dogmas. Yet all Jewish systems prior to the nineteenth century lay down dogmas. Therefore, if the word Jewish is properly applied only to a belief identical with that of the past, we have the absurd result that in the phrase "Polydox Jewish theology" the term "Polydox" would allow beliefs that the term "Jewish" would forbid. The term "Polydox" would expand and affirm freedom; the term "Jewish" would constrict and deny freedom.

The third reason is that it is not possible in actual practice to apply the static rule. The static rule calls for the name Jewish to be applied to a theology in the present that is identical with theology called Jewish in the past. A sine qua non of this rule, then, is that there is a single past theology called Jewish to serve as the criterion of application. The past as investigated by the critical study of Judaism, however, does not give us a single Jewish theology, rather it gives us many theologies and God concepts that have been called Jewish, not a few of which differ substantially from one another. What is the standard we will use to determine which of these many past Jewish theologies should serve as the criterion for our use of the term Jewish? Will it be the theology and God concept of Amos, based upon original prophetic experience, which differs greatly from the theology of the Pharisees, based upon the tradition of a perfect and finished revelation to Moses? Yet both differ radically from Maimonides' concept of God, based as it is on negative theology and the primacy of reason. These examples can be multiplied tens of times. What has the theology of Mendelssohn to do with the Kabbala, both of which are called Jewish? Hence it is impossible, except arbitrarily, to select a past Jewish theology which shall define our use of the term Jewish and serve as the paradigm par excellence for application of the static rule.[13]

Essence of Judaism Rejected

One further observation concerning the static rule: there is a procedure that masquerades as the application of this rule, but which upon inspection turns out to be just the contrary. This procedure by abstraction attempts to bring in the static rule through the rear door. The argument is given that all theology called Jewish in the past has an essence which can be abstracted, as, for example, monotheism, and that the word Jewish, therefore, is properly applied only to a theology that has this monotheistic characteristic. But the static rule requires identity between a past and present theology. Those who abstract a concept such as monotheism from complex theological systems such as those that constitute the Jewish religious past, and maintain that such a general monotheism is their essence, do not apply the past, they violate it. They improperly introduce an entirely new theology, general monotheism. Take the following case as an illustration. To the Pharisees and their Orthodox descendants, the name Jewish is not applied to a theology because it is monotheistic; the theologies of Christianity and Islam are monotheistic too. The name Jewish is applied to a theology that consists of a *particular* kind of monotheism and affirms a *particular* revelation. Hence to generalize away the particular Pharisaic monotheism and revelation is not to keep the past and apply the static rule, but on the contrary, to repudiate the past and change the very essence of Pharisaic Judaism.

Moreover, abstraction as a name-giving principle does not work. If we say that the word Jewish is applied to a theology simply because it is monotheistic, then Christian, Islamic, and many other theologies are Jewish. Surely, this is absurd. We are seeking a principle that will enable us to apply the name Jewish to theology more accurately, but we find that abstraction destroys whatever meaning the phrase Jewish theology may reasonably and ordinarily be understood to have. In other words, a rule based upon abstraction or "essence" that would be broad enough to include the entire Jewish theological past would be so broad that theologies would be included that are plainly not Jewish.

Ontal Symbol—Dynamic Meaning of the Word Jew

Inasmuch as the static meaning of the word Jewish cannot be applied, another meaning is here proposed for the word Jewish in the phrase "Polydox Jewish theology."[14] This meaning, which is open to change and progress, may be said to be implicit in some instances of past usage, but is not identical with any meaning of the past consciously given. We will term this use the *dynamic meaning of the word Jewish.*

The dynamic meaning is based upon a theory of the word Jew as an ontal symbol.[15] This theory is based upon the phenomenology of the human person presented above as a problem finite existent.[16] The sense of the term *problem* as employed here is pointed to by its etymology. *Problema* in Greek means "something thrown forward," that is, a question that is proposed for solution. The existence of the human person is not given to the person as a closed and completed thing, fully and at one time, but is thrown forward as a question of concerned interest demanding solution. The human person cannot refuse to ask this question, although it engenders angst, for she or he is the question that is asked. This question is: "I am finite, I crave infinity, what can I do, what should I do, what will I do?" The conflict between the finite being of human persons and the infinite strivings of their will is sharp, penetrating to the core of the human personality and a threat to its unity and integrity. Finity entails aloneness and death, whereas the infinite will desires unlimited being and eternity. The response of human persons to the conflict between what they essentially are and what they desire to be—in other words, their response to the conflict of finitude—has been described as the definition of religion. *An ontal symbol is a symbol that points to the problem structure of the human being (ontos), that is, to the conflict of finitude, and summons the human to respond to the problem and resolve it with authenticity.*[17] The word Jew has the power to serve as an ontal symbol. As an ontal symbol the word Jew turns the one whom it names to the essential demand of her or his being; but as an ontal symbol, it summons only to authentic response, it does not call for some one particular response.[18] In a religious situation such as Polydox Judaism, where the evidence for response is admittedly fallible, and the autonomy of each adherent affirmed, response is determined as authentic not by its agreement with the past or with dogma, but by the competence of the response in resolving the individual conflict of finitude of the one who makes it.

The ontal symbol Jew brings before the one who bears the name past and present possibilities of response. The possibilities produced by the past are evoked by the intrinsic association of the word Jew with the history that produced it: Shall it be decided with the pentateuchal Jew that no Infinite intervenes in the structure of finite being, and that human existence is inexorably bounded by the limit of death? Or shall it be decided with the Pharisaic Jew that relation to an Infinite breaches the limits of finity and grants an afterlife? The possibilities of the present are evoked by the word Jew as the name of a "now existent" whom it calls to authentic response.[19] For the response of the "now existent" takes place in a concrete present reality to which, if the response is to be authentic, it must have the right to be true.

A Polydox Definition of Jewish Theology

Thus the meaning of the word Jew as ontal symbol is dynamic; it is not bound to the past as the static meaning is; it is heuristic, furthering investigation into the nature of humankind and its

universe. Here lies the relation between the word Jew and dynamic theology. As an ontal symbol, the word Jew creates theology, and the creation is therefore properly named after that
which begets it. The ontal symbol creates ideology by inducing
those to whom it calls to search for authentic response to their
conflict of finitude. Authentic response is based on reality, and a
concept of God, the product of theology, gives to the one who
accepts it characteristics of the real ultimately relevant to her or
his finite condition. The conflict of finitude, it may be said, raises
the question of the infinite; theology provides the intellectual
answer; religion is the existential response. A definition of Jewish
theology appropriate for a polydoxy is therefore *the study of the
meaning of the word God produced by the finite being named
Jew who is called by her or his name to give an authentic
response to the conflict of finitude.*

God

We come then to our final subject, the word *God*. Inasmuch as
no authoritative or dogmatic definition of God can be laid down
in a polydoxy—more than one view with respect to the word
God is consistent with a polydoxy's essence—the discussion that
follows is to be regarded primarily as an explanation of why the
author takes the position he does, rather than as a polemic
against positions to which others are committed and which possess great value for them. Of course, in explaining why any position is taken, it is inevitable that reasons should be given why
other positions have been rejected; negation is an aspect of affirmation. Negation, however, is not the purpose of this exposition, and it is only incidental to the spirit in which it is presented.

Justification and Evidence

All inquiry into the reality and nature of a professed existent
begins with an examination of the ways of knowing.[20] Even our
brief investigation, therefore, cannot proceed directly to a state-

ment of the reality and nature of God. Rather, as all theology must, it starts with a consideration of the nature of evidence and the justification of belief. What is the evidence, if any, that is necessary to justify belief in a reality called God?

To begin with, let us consider the possibility that no evidence at all is to be required. It is evident that no proof can be brought to determine the question of evidence, inasmuch as that which constitutes a proof is itself dependent upon the same question. No proof, therefore, can be brought that evidence is necessary; the choice of evidence is a starting point of inquiry. One who wishes can without evidence state anything, affirm anything, or believe anything. Such is the way of ipse dixit theology. Having conceded this, however, the choice here is that evidence must be given to justify whatever reality reference is to be assigned the word God. There is no quarrel with those who use their freedom to deny that evidence is necessary, provided that they affirm the freedom of others to withhold serious consideration from any proposed reality meaning of God for which no evidence is given. The word theology literally means "science or knowledge of God," and though the heart may not wish to know, thought must have its reasons. As Maimonides says in laying down the rules of evidence and faith which preface his inquiry into the nature of God:

> [B]ear in mind that by "faith" we do not mean that which is uttered with the lips, but that which is apprehended by the [rational] soul, the conviction that the object [of belief] is exactly as it is conceived. If, as regards real or supposed truths, you content yourself with giving utterance to them in words, without conceiving them or believing in them, especially if you do not seek certainty, you have a very easy task, as, in fact, you will find many ignorant people who retain [the words of] beliefs [in their memory] without conceiving any idea with regard to them. . . belief is only possible after a thing is conceived; it consists in the conviction that the thing apprehended has its existence beyond the mind [in reality] exactly as it is conceived in the mind. . . . Renounce desires and habits, follow your reason. . . you will then be fully convinced of what we have said. . . .[21]

Without evidence, there is no conviction possible for the human person, the existent who, perhaps *malgré lui,* is reality committed and rationally endowed.

Subjective Evidence Theology

The decision having been made that evidence is necessary to establish a reality reference for the word God, we must now weigh which of the two kinds of evidence generally accepted is to be required, subjective or objective. The outstanding characteristic of our age regarding theological evidence is that the objective evidence that has in the past been employed to justify faith in a reality reference for the word God is now generally rejected, and particularly is this the case among liberal religions. This is primarily the evidence described above under the first form of theology, infallible and authoritative revelation. But repudiated as well is the evidence of infallible and authoritative natural knowledge, described above under the second form of theology. The most striking consequence of this development is that the evidence that traditionally provided the substantiation of the concept of God that has been referred to as theistic absolutism has been discarded. Theistic absolutism, which among Jewish religions is subscribed to in its most rigorous form by Pharisaic or Orthodox Judaism, is, as stated earlier, the theory that the referent of the word God is an omniscient, omnipotent, omnibenevolent being who reveals himself to humans.[22] Those who reject the traditional evidence and wish to retain theistic absolutism must now resort to subjective evidence, which constitutes theology of the fourth form, since no theology of the fifth form satisfactorily makes a case for this concept.[23] Hence those theologians who vigorously affirm the validity of subjective evidence are primarily the ones who are equally committed to the concept of theistic absolutism. Owing to this present, intimate relation between subjective evidence and theistic absolutism, it is difficult and abstract to evaluate subjective evidence without touching on the latter as well. We find a good description of the mode of subjective evidence predominantly subscribed to today, apprehension of a "presence," in the following:

> The new and more empiricist apologetic that is replacing the traditional theistic proofs focuses attention upon the state of religious faith, and claims that this is a state which it is rational to be in, but which philosophical reasoning cannot put one in.
>
> The state of faith, in its strongest instances, is that of someone who cannot help believing in God.[24] He reports that he is conscious of God—not of course as an object in the world, but as a divine presence. In the Old Testament, for example, the prophets were aware of God as dealing with Israel through the vicissitudes of her national history. In the New Testament the disciples were conscious of God as acting towards them in and through Jesus, so that His attitudes towards the various men and women whom He met were God's attitudes towards those same people. And the contemporary man of faith is aware of existing in the unseen presence of God and of living his life within the sphere of a universal divine purpose.
>
> Having thus pointed to a putative religious awareness, the new apologetic argues that this is no more in need of a philosophical proof of the reality of its object than is our perception of the physical world or of other people. The rationalist assumption is no more valid in relation to religious cognition than in relation to sense experience. . . . [T]he believer does not reason from his religious experience to God but is conscious of God Himself. . . . The central claim of the new type of apologetic is that it is rational for someone who believes himself to be aware of God, and who finds himself linked in this belief with a long-lived community of faith, to trust his religious awareness and to proceed to base his life upon it.[25]

Critique of Subjective Evidence

Inasmuch as the points usually made in favor of subjective evidence as the basis of theology are ably summarized in these comments, an analysis of their contents will serve as a critique of subjective evidence generally.[26] If subjective evidence is found wanting by this critique, as I believe it is, then no alternative is left but to select objective evidence of the fifth form as the justification necessary to establish a reality reference for the word God.

1. Once the principle is affirmed that subjective evidence is valid, then the subjective evidence of every person is validated. If everyone's subjective evidence is valid, how is a choice to be made between two conflicting statements on the nature of God and religion, both of which are supported by subjective evidence? How does one choose between the God and religion of the Pentateuch, which knows of no Trinity, Messiah, resurrection, or immortality, and the God and religion of fundamentalist Christianity, which affirms the Trinity, a Messiah, and makes afterlife the goal and purpose of human existence? Surely, unless reason and the law of contradiction are to be dismissed, these religions cannot both be correct.[27] It is possible, we may suppose, for a person to claim that her or his subjective evidence testifies to its own validity and tells as well which other subjective evidence is valid. But this seems rather arbitrary and unconvincing. It is equivalent, in fact, to a claim of prophecy. Subjective evidence, then, does not seem to provide a much better criterion for determining truth than no evidence at all. One of the principal reasons for requiring evidence is to judge between truth claims, but the theology of subjective evidence seems to serve this purpose no better than ipse dixit theology.

2. Furthermore, if the believer "is conscious of God Himself," how is it, for example, that the preexilic prophets' and Jesus' concepts of the nature of God differ so? And why does the Muslim experience Allah; the Christian, Jesus; and the Hindu, Brahma? The analogy between religious cognition and sense perception is surely farfetched. Few will disagree, I am sure, that the tree the prophet sees will answer to Jesus' notion of a tree, and to ours as well, yet for people ostensibly experiencing the same "presence," their notions of deity and religion differ greatly indeed.

3. One of the conclusions of Sigmund Freud's investigations was that the experience of "presence" which some take as meeting with the deity is properly understood as an experience of self objectified and projected outward. How, in this Freudian and

scientific age, can it be considered "rational" to accept the mere fact of experiencing a "presence" as consciousness of "God Himself"? Rather, it would appear that one of the prime methodological considerations in a theology competent for our time is the recognition that "presences" per se can well be projections of the unconscious.

4. The concept of God that the experience of "presence" is usually taken to substantiate is theistic absolutism. This is the concept of a being whose nature has consequences for the world we experience. A universe created and governed by an omniscient, omnipotent, and omnibenevolent being may be expected to display the marks of a perfect source. Thus the apprehension of "presence" is clearly not adequate by itself to demonstrate the truth of this concept; it must be proved coherent with the facts of the universe as well. We can all grant that there are those who encounter "presences"; the problem is the world of brute fact. Many of our experiences in the world of brute fact are incoherent with theistic absolutism, the most critical of which is the experience of surd evil. If the facts could be brought into harmony with the concept of theistic absolutism, "presence" theology would have little difficulty in making its point.[28] Yet the medievals, who considered their concept of God supported by indubitable evidence, gave more attention to its congruence with the external world than theologians today whose primary evidence is the ambiguous "presence."

The conclusion from these considerations is that subjective evidence does not convincingly establish a real being, a reality reference for the word God. Before leaving the subject of subjective evidence, however, three points should be stressed. First, repeating the opinion stated earlier, theology based upon subjective evidence is appropriate to Polydox Judaism only if such theology is understood to be nonauthoritative.[29] Second, the use of "presence" is only objected to as primary evidence for a concept of deity; no objection is made to the use of "presence" as corroborative evidence for a divine reality established by objective means, or as a symbol referring to a reality so established. Third, not all forms of theism are established by subjective evidence; the exponents of theistic finitism, for example, appeal in the main to objective evidence.[30]

Objective Evidence Theology

The form of theology to which we now come is the pursuit of a reality reference for God based on objective evidence of the kind earlier classified as theology of the fifth form. For many, the primary difficulty regarding this form of theology is that the objective evidence presently available does not substantiate the concept of theistic absolutism. Their disappointment is understandable, but no rebuttal of truth. Those who require objective evidence employ a strict standard of evidence precisely because they are aware of the human person's infinite strivings and the screen they often place between the person and reality. Genuine religion is to have one's view of the word God shape one's emotions and desires, and not the contrary. Thus, far from being that which religion should avoid, reality objectively determined provides the basis of true religion and ultimate meaningful existence. For authentic response to finitude, which constitutes true religion, must be based upon reality, and ultimate meaningful existence is nothing other than the state such response produces.

Moreover, while subjective theology is consistent with the essence of Polydox Judaism, objective theology is more than consistent; it is also coherent, fitting naturally with the origins and spirit of polydoxy. Polydoxy came into existence as a result of the conclusion that Scripture is fallible, the work, at least in part, of humans.[31] This conclusion was arrived at through critical and objective study, scientific inquiry applied to Scripture. Is it not natural to apply this same method to the theology of Polydox Judaism as well?

Enduring Possibility of Being

There are several theories of truth based upon objective evidence. Since it would take us far afield to enter upon the intricacies of reflection involved in selecting one theory over another, it will suffice for our purpose merely to indicate the one to which the author subscribes. This is the theory that a proposition concerning the external world is true if it is empirically verifiable. This does not mean, as those who generally subscribe to empirical verifiability as the criterion of truth maintain, that there is no knowledge of one's self. That such knowledge is held to be possible is clear, inasmuch as it is the knowledge on which the ontal symbol and authentic response to the conflict of finitude are based. However, empirical verifiability is prescribed as the arbiter of truth concerning the external world, and seeing that God as a real being is a fact of the external world, a theory of truth regarding deity must be one that pertains to knowledge of this world.

A brief formulation of the notion of empirical verifiability can be stated thusly: "A proposition or series of propositions concerning the external world will be true if there are predictable and observable consequences of such a proposition or propositions." Hence the test that a definition of God must meet is empirical verifiability. If there are empirical consequences of the definition, then the proposition *God exists* will be true, and if there are not, the proposition will be meaningless or false. The definition of God I propose, consequently, is the following: *God is the enduring possibility of being.* By *being* is meant selfa (or self-data) and sensa (or sense-data).[32] Inasmuch as being is analyzable without remainder into selfa and sensa, the existence of God is verified whenever selfa and sensa can both be experienced, and the existence of God is disproved when, under equivalent conditions of personal normalcy, selfa are experienced and sensa no longer are. God is disproved as the enduring possibility of being rather than as the enduring possibility of sense experience alone because the person (that is, the continuing self-consciousness that is constructed out of selfa)[33] is evidently dependent upon the external world (sensa and the unobservables reducible to sensa), and with the annihilation of the external world, the inexorable annihilation of the person may be inferred.

Hylotheism

The definition of God as the enduring possibility of being is a concept of God called *hylotheism*.[34] Hylotheism belongs to the class of concepts that may generally be subsumed under the heading of *finite God concepts*. Quite different theologies are grouped together under this heading but they all possess the common characteristic that deity is not regarded as perfect, judging "perfection" by the largely imaginary and arbitrary standard of "possessing every desirable attribute." For the most part, the imperfection attributed to deity in finite God concepts relates to the inability of God to overcome the force of evil. In the view of deity as the enduring possibility of being, the divine imperfection goes beyond this, to the essential nature of the divine existence.

The Possible, the Actual, and Nothingness

Two classes of existence, each with its distinctive nature, can be distinguished: the *possible* and the *actual*. Possible existence suffers this defect: it lacks actuality. As possibility, it is neither a selfum nor a sensum. Yet if the divine existence is to be of lasting duration,[35] it can accomplish this only as possibility. For the actually existent is always limited; nothing unlimited can be experienced or imagined, let alone conceived. Hence to be actual is to be finite. While the finity of every actuality is present in all the spheres of its existence, it is temporal finity that provides the definitive boundary. The actual is finite in time because, as an actuality, it is finite in the power of existence and destined therefore, as an individual, to annihilation. Being thus breeds nothingness; indeed, *nothing* has no meaning except in relation to being. Accordingly, if God is to be of lasting duration, the divine existence must forego actuality for possibility. We find therefore that God is of lasting duration, but possesses only possible existence, whereas being is finite in duration, but possesses actual existence.

Metaphorically speaking, existence, the act of overcoming nothingness, lays down conditions on all that would possess it. As a consequence, nothingness is never entirely overcome. Actual existents temporarily overcome nothingness at the cost of future and total annihilation. God overcomes nothingness by incorporating it into the divine existence, and, in so doing, is emptied of actuality and must forever remain possibility. The divine existence, so to speak, is a compromise between being and nothingness; the ground of being overcomes nothingness to exist as the enduring possibility of being, but in the uneasy victory defect is assimilated into the Godhead.

God and the World

The status of God's existence as the enduring possibility of being leads to a further consequence: God cannot exist without the world. God has no meaning without being; being has no endurance without God. God's existence is not absolute; the enduring possibility of being exists as a correlative of being. The world was not created by an absolute God who arbitrarily willed it so; rather the world exists because the divine existence is unconditionally dependent upon it. Of creation *ex nihilo,* we have no knowledge. In experience, God coexists with finites in a process of continuous interaction. In this process, as we are justified in concluding from the regular and orderly nature of causal sequence, the possibility of future being is derived from present being. In other words, the existence of God is derived from every present moment of being and realized in every future moment. God is the ground of being and being is the ground of God.

God, Humankind, and Covenant

A further consequence of God's nature as possibility is the relation that obtains between God and humankind. In this view of God, where the divine is subject to the conditions of existence, it is the nature of actual entities, by virtue of the finity or encompassing boundary that gives them their existence, to be cut off from the ground of their being. To be actual is to be alone. To be finite is to be severed from the enduring. Hence the relation between God and humankind is one of muted communication. Accordingly, as polydoxy teaches, there exists no infallible or verbal revelation, nor can there be such revelation, because humankind, necessarily and substantially separated from the ground of being, has no sure relation to this ground. Equally, the perfect providence of theistic absolutism, its Messiahs and supernatural eschatologies, have no place in a world where the enduring exists only as a possibility and the actual world is always finite. Yet if God cannot overcome human finity, humans are not powerless. The possibilities that constitute the Godhead can be influenced and even altered by humankind. Every ontal decision that resolves the pain of finitude increases the possibility of pleasurable being in the future; every social decision that helps resolve the pain of injustice and poverty increases the possibility of social betterment in the future; every scientific discovery becomes a power for the future. If humans will the good, God conserves all the value that is possible.

This relation of action and passion between humankind and God may be viewed symbolically as a covenant, an ethics of hypothetical necessity: If the human person acts, then God reacts; and, as the human person acts, so God reacts. In the words of the prophet Amos:

> Seek good, and not evil, that ye may live;
> And so the Lord, the God of hosts,
> will be with you, as ye say.
> Hate the evil, and love the good,
> and establish justice in the gate. (Amos 5:14 f)

This covenant, in which the human person must do the good to receive the good, is to be sharply distinguished from supernatural covenants with deity, in which the person is required to perform some act irrelevant to the good, ritualistic or otherwise, and God, without prior and competent natural causes, miraculously produces the good.

Hylotheism and the Problem of Evil

The absence of an infallible and verbal revelation is only part of the larger problem of evil, the great complex of events and conditions that beset and anguish human existence. Evil comes from events outside the human person and from conditions within. The human person, in attempting to cope with the problems the self and world present, is not only inherently deficient intellectually, lacking certainty in knowledge and absolutes in ethics, but is constitutionally deficient emotionally and physically as well. These lacks keep the person from perfect and permanent solutions to ultimate problems, and provide constant threats to the very meaning of existence. In no way can evil be accounted for satisfactorily by theological absolutism. This includes not only theistic absolutism, but pantheistic absolutism as well, such as we find, for example, in Spinozism. The Whole that is the Spinozistic substance cannot contain the evils of the world and be coherently pronounced perfect any more than a theistic omniscient, omnipotent, and omnibenevolent Creator can be coherently pronounced perfect. The Whole exists in and through its parts and cannot escape the defects of their nature, just as the absolute Creator is responsible for his creatures and cannot escape the consequences of their acts.

In the theology of divine possibility, there is a coherent explanation of evil. Evil is the inevitable result of the nature of a God that can only exist as possibility and the nature of humans who can only exist as finite. Evil is not willed into existence; it is a necessary concomitant of existence. The choice, figuratively stated, is not between a world with evil and a world without it, but between a world with evil and no world at all.

Thus two principles in the theology of divine possibility serve to explain evil. The first is that all actual being is necessarily finite. Every actual thing will in every way be limited; being does not endure. This does not mean that meliorism is unrealistic and melioration cannot occur—it can and does—but melioration is all that can occur. No final triumph over limitation and nothingness is possible. The second principle is that God, the divine possibility, can only offer for realization in the future the possibilities that reside in the being of the present. God, in other words, is not an independent and absolute agent who can miraculously produce the good *ex nihilo;* the divine existence can present for realization in the future only that which has been made possible in the past. Together, these two principles, that the "present" or world of actualities is always limited, and that the future can only be created out of possibilities derived from a present that is limited, offer an explanation of the pervasive occurrence of evil in the world.

Hylotheism and Polydoxy

The theology of divine possibility is offered as a theology appropriate and coherent with a polydoxy. Out of their freedom polydoxians may accept or reject it. A theology should, however, only be rejected on valid grounds; and there is one objection that is not valid. This objection argues that a theology must satisfy the infinite wishes of humans and provide them with unlimited consolation. This argument is invalid because it is based upon a mistaken conception of theology in particular and of religion in general. The purpose of theology is truth and the purpose of religion is to enable the human person to live authentically with that truth. Hence truth is the only relevant and necessary justification of a theology.

As Maimonides so profoundly taught, a theology is as important for that which it negates as for that which it affirms.[36] The worshp of false gods is idolatry, and if a theology should serve to keep humans from idolatry, even though, as in the case of Maimonides' theology, it should tell them nothing of the essence of God, then such a theology will have accomplished a great good. Throughout history, there has been a special fury attached to the deeds of those who have acted in the name of false gods, and who have rationalized through idolatry despotic and tyrannical urges that were solely their own. The theology of divine possibility as a negative theology serves the moral role of denying divinity to any finite, no matter the basis upon which the divinity is claimed, whether through revelation or incarnation. The fact of evil, resulting as it does from the necessary limitations of existence, should not bring us to despair, but to the meaningful awareness that the divine possibility reacts to acts of value and conserves all possible good. Yet there is an austere overtone to the concept of God as possibility. As possibility, God does not produce the concrete realization of human good; this of necessity is left to humankind. Should humans in this critical age fail, then we must be aware with Amos and the author of the Noah story that God does not require for his existence any particular people, species, or world. While it is true that God without any world at all has no existence, the divine enduring possibility does not require any particular world or class of finites for existence. The awesome choice, whether humans are to be included in an existing class of finites, is left at this point in time to humankind itself.

Notes

1. For a definition of Polydox Judaism, see pp. 46 ff.

2. As, e.g., Polydox Reform Judaism, and *mutatis mutandis,* Polydox Christianity, universal Polydoxy, and, generally, the analogue religions of Reform Judaism; see p. 14.

3. F. Heer points out that Christians before Abelard avoided the word theology owing to its associations with pagan antiquity; *The Medieval World* (London, 1962), p. 21.

4. As previously noted, the books of the Pentateuch and Prophets do not contain the term Jew.

5. The term *atom* is a case in point. In Greek philosophy, the word

refers to an indivisible particle. In contemporary science, it refers to an entity that can be split and is divisible into smaller particles. No one faults science for retaining the term atom and giving it a new meaning that is the opposite of what it meant originally.

6. E.g., Abraham Cronbach, *Realities of Religion* (New York, 1957), pp. 31-49.

7. See pp. 85 f.

8. M. Buber, *I and Thou,* pp. 56 ff., *et al.* (N.Y., 1970). It should be noted that Buber rejects the term "experience" for the I-Thou relation.

9. See pp. 84 f.

10. The analysis given here of the term *Jewish* applies equally to the term *Christian.*

11. For the same reasons, the static rule cannot be applied in Reform and Reconstructionist Judaisms.

12. Similarly, Reform and Reconstructionist Judaisms by the fact of their existence repudiate the static rule.

13. It is interesting to note that the totality of the Jewish theological past, as revealed by the science of Judaism, is itself pluralistic, containing varied and mutually exclusive theologies. Only Polydox Judaism in the present can offer the entire past (within the broad limits set by the logic of polydoxy) as possibilities for choice and decision.

14. This meaning is also suitable for Reform Judaism and Reconstructionist Judaism.

15. Words other than *Jew* can serve as ontal symbols. The word *Christian* is one, and in the author's opinion has often functioned as one, particularly in the modern age. The word *philosopher* has also functioned as an ontal symbol.

16. See pp. 59 ff.

17. See pp. 63 ff.

18. The meaning of the word Jew as ontal symbol can and does coexist with other possible meanings of the word, ethnic, political, and so forth. Individual Jews determine which meaning or meanings may be significant to them.

19. A "now existent" is a person living in a present that offers contemporaneous views of ultimate reality, as opposed to those views transmitted to a "now existent" from the past.

20. Compare the discussion of the words *belief* and *faith* given on pp. 83 ff.

21. *The Guide of the Perplexed,* I, 50.

22. Revelation is, I think, implicit in the most rigorous form of theistic absolutism. Strictly speaking, theistic absolutism does not entail a revelation.

23. Neither does all evidence of the fourth term verify theistic absolutism; the Buberian "I-Thou," e.g., does not; neither does mystic union.

24. By "God" here is meant theistic absolutism.

25. John H. Hick, *Saturday Evening Review,* February 6, 1965.

26. The Buberian "I-Thou" relation is subject to similar (as well as other) criticism, but requires special consideration which cannot be given here.

27. It might be argued that this is the same theistic absolutistic God revealing himself to people in different guises. But it contradicts the concept of a theistic absolutistic God for him to reveal to different people mutually exclusive descriptions of his nature, for only one can be true, and God, therefore, would, in all but one case of revelation, be the revealer of untruth. Another objection (and there are many) is that it would contradict the omnibenevolent nature of the theistic absolutistic God to foment strife among humans, but controversy over the truth of revelation claims has been the focal point of history's many religious wars and persecutions.

28. "Presence" theology has on its side the fact that the concept of God it wishes to establish allows the most pleasurable or least demanding response to finitude. Of all concepts of God, none provides more security and comfort for a finite being.

29. It is difficult to see how in any religion subjective evidence can reasonably be taken to be authoritative.

30. See E. S. Brightman, *A Philosophy of Religion* (New York, 1940), pp. 189 ff.

31. Reform Judaism likewise came into existence for this reason.

32. The singular forms are selfum (or self-datum) and sensum (or sense-datum).

33. The sense of continuity to self-consciousness is provided by memory. Each selfum is discrete, as is each sensum.

34. Hylotheism is the doctrine that matter is God. Matter here is used in its original sense of potentiality or possibility, not in the sense of body.

35. But not necessarily of infinite or everlasting duration.

36. *The Guide of the Perplexed,* I, 58.

37. One additional point remains to be made concerning hylotheism. In theologies generally, however they may differ, there is the notion that the existence of deity is absolutely assured, and deity is, therefore, "eternal" or "everlasting." In hylotheism, the existence of deity is not assured, and deity can conceivably go out of existence, and with it all being, if the evidence of an empirical, that is, scientific cosmology, were to require this. At this time, the non-existence of deity is not required by empirical cosmology, but it does require its value equivalent: the future death of all that is valuable by reasonable human standards. The universe either is open or closed. If the universe is open, it will reach an ultimate condition of unending meaningless cold and darkness. If the universe is closed, it will enter into an unending meaningless cycle of the utter destruction of all that is valuable followed by a new explosion of existence for which the same fate awaits. At this time, the evidence of scientific cosmology supports the view that the universe is open; W. Sullivan, *Black Holes* (New York, 1979), pp. 267 f. It may be noted in this context that for the hylotheist the appropriate response to the conflict of finitude whereby soteria is achieved is the finite response; see above, pp. 70 ff.

Chapter VII

Providence, Hylotheism, and a Theology of Jewish Survival

Jews and the Jewish Religious Complex

It has been made clear that the term *Jew* has no one meaning and can be understood, consequently, in a variety of different senses. It is necessary, therefore, to begin with a description of the way it will be employed here. The term *Jew* will refer to persons for whom it is a name that is primarily of religious significance.[1] Persons for whom the name has primarily religious significance have historically, however, adhered to a number of different religious systems; that is, various groups of Jews have subscribed to different religions. These different religious systems are referred to as *Jewish religious systems* or *Jewish religions*. To refer to the totality of Jewish religious systems, no matter the degree to which they have differed or do differ from one another, the term *Jewish religious complex* has been employed.[2] The Jewish religious complex will be considered as surviving if even just one Jewish religion exists. The subject to be examined in this exposition of a theology of Jewish survival is the survival of the Jewish religious complex.

Theories of Providence

Theologically, the question of the survival of the Jewish religious complex fundamentally concerns the form of providence to which Jews are subject, for without Jews there can be no Jewish religious complex. By providence is meant the cause or system of causes that produces and/or sustains an actuality.[3] Hence the survival of the Jewish religious complex is dependent upon a providence or causal ground that governs the existence of Jews. Over the ages traversed by the Jewish religious complex, varying theories of providence, some mutually exclusive, have been advanced regarding the survival of Jews. A classification of these theories, from a logical rather than historical point of view, will be helpful in clarifying the issue before us. The general categories into which the theories of providence may be divided, according to their fundamental characteristics relevant to this inquiry, are the following: *metaphenomenal* and *phenomenal, conditional* and *absolute, individual* and *collective, eternal* and *temporal, special* and *universal,* and *static* and *dynamic.*

Metaphenomenal and Phenomenal Providence

Perhaps no greater distinction between theories of providence exists than that between the metaphenomenal and phenomenal. An actuality that is subject to metaphenomenal providence is one whose existence is determined by an extraordinary order of causation, outside the phenomenal order. On the other hand, the actuality governed by phenomenal providence receives its existence from the causal order of the observable universe, an order whose manifestations and regularities can be determined with more or less precision by the physical or social sciences, and such an actuality possesses no causation beyond the observation, verification, or scope of these sciences. The sense of the phrase "phenomenal providence" is theologically and metaphysically neutral. To affirm that an actuality is subject to phenomenal providence is to say nothing about any entity outside such providence that might be understood or conjectured as underlying the order of causation to which it refers, and which is ultimately taken to account for this order. Accordingly, the force of the phrase "phenomenal providence"is phenomenological, involving no commitment to or against a ground beyond the order to which it refers. In a disagreement, therefore, over whether some actuality is subject to metaphenomenal or phenomenal providence, the issue is not necessarily belief in a personal deity; one may believe in a personal deity and still maintain humankind is subject to phenomenal providence alone. Maimonides,[4] and particularly deists, believe in a personal deity and maintain that humans are subject to phenomenal providence alone. Similarly, the sense of "metaphenomenal providence" is phenomenological, referring to extraordinary causation, and it is neutral with respect to the ultimate source of that causation. In the Jewish religious complex, however, such extraordinary causation has usually been understood theistically, as proceeding from a personal being who supernaturally governs the universe.

The categories of "metaphenomenal" and "phenomenal providence" are to be distinguished from those of "supernatural" and "natural providence" whose meanings they somewhat resemble. The former have been introduced to avoid certain theological or metaphysical connotations frequently associated with the latter. Thus the distinction between supernatural and natural providence has often been understood as that which exists between providence in a universe where there is a being named "God" and providence in a universe where no such being exists, or between a providence that has religious value and one that does not. No such connotations should be associated with the distinction between the categories of metaphenomenal and phenomenal providence. Whereas it is most usually the case that one who affirms a metaphenomenal providence will at the same time affirm a referent named God, this is not always so. Similarly, it is not necessarily the case that one who affirms a phenomenal providence will negate such a referent, and, as has been noted, this referent may even be a God who is a person.

With the exception of the medieval philosophic tradition, the various systems of the Jewish religious complex, until the modern age, have universally viewed the survival of Jewish existence as governed by metaphenomenal providence. The precise nature of this providence, however, as will appear in the course of investigating the other categories, has been understood by these systems in essentially different ways, from collective survival in earthly life alone,[5] to both collective and individual survival in an afterlife as well.[6] It may be added, too, that in some systems, Jewish survival is viewed as subject to both metaphenomenal and phenomenal providence. This is most clearly seen in the case of those medieval and modernist philosophic theologians who distinguish between the special and general wills of God, the former referring to his action of producing miracles, and the latter to his action of sustaining the natural order. Still, a providence so divided cannot eternally stand, and ultimately in the case of such double providence systems one or the other form prevails and becomes the sole determinant of existence.[7]

Conditional and Absolute Providence

The distinction between the categories of conditional and absolute providence is drawn by the end of the biblical period. Conditional providence is a system of causation in which the causal ground sustains an actuality if and only if the actuality meets certain terms or conditions. Annihilation is the penalty for failure to fulfill the stipulations. Under absolute providence, existence is received from the causal ground unilaterally and unconditionally, regardless of the actuality's actions. The concepts of absolute and conditional providence have both been subscribed to by Jews. Among those who subscribe to the latter, different and mutually exclusive conditions for Jewish existence have been proposed. Notable among these are: morality, which was emphasized particularly by the preexilic prophets; creed and ritual, which were stressed by the Pentateuch and the Pharisees; and knowledge of metaphysics and science required by the Jewish philosophic tradition. Only among the preexilic prophets, however, does it seem that the annihilation of the Jews in their entirety for failure to meet the conditions of existence was a real possibility. The reasons given for Jewish existence enjoying absolute providence have always been based upon a theistic theology and include the following beliefs (stressed particularly by the post-exilic prophets): Yahveh has arbitrarily chosen the Jews as his special people and possesses an undying, protective love for them; the Jews have undergone historical experiences which make them alone competent to bear witness to and teach Yahveh's cardinal truth, that Yahveh is the god of all humankind; and that Yahveh, after long, special association with the Jews, cannot sever the relationship without injury to his reputation or good name.

Individual and Collective Providence

The distinction between individual and collective providence arises in those systems that distinguish the causal ground supporting an individual actuality from that supporting a collectivity. This distinction takes various forms in the Jewish religious complex. According to Amos, and in preexilic prophecy generally, the Jewish collectivity receives metaphenomenal providence, including retributive justice, whereas the fate of the individual person is determined by chance and the fate of the collectivity of which the person is part. In post-exilic Judaism, and particularly in Pharisaism, the individual as well as the collectivity receives metaphenomenal providence and just retribution. The distinction between individual and collective providence occurs even in phenomenal systems of providence. Thus Maimonides is of the opinion that the human species receives unconditional providence whereas the individual person receives conditional providence alone.

Eternal and Temporal Providence

The categories of eternal and temporal providence are distinguished this way: In eternal providence the causal ground either absolutely or conditionally provides eternal existence to the actuality it governs, so that the actuality need not, therefore, suffer non-existence.[8] But in temporal providence, the actuality receives only limited or temporary existence from the causal ground. Radically different positions have been taken in the Jewish religious complex on the question of eternal and temporal providence. In the biblical period, there was universal agreement that there was no eternal providence for the individual, but opinions varied regarding the Jewish collectivity. The preexilic prophets, we may infer, believed that eternal providence for the Jewish collectivity was possible if the necessary conditions were met, whereas the post-exilic prophets maintained that eternal providence for the collectivity was not only possible, but unconditionally assured as well. According to Pharisaism, on the other hand, Jewish individuals and the collectivity alike enjoyed eternal providence. It should be noted that the fact that a system of providence is metaphenomenal does not mean it will also be eternal, as may be seen from the providence systems of the biblical period, in which individual persons never receive eternal existence. By the same token, a system being phenomenal does not mean it cannot or does not provide eternity, as in the case of Maimonides, who affirmed a phenomenal providence yet believed that the Intelligences and celestial spheres as well as all terrestrial species receive eternal providence.

Special and Universal Providence

The distinction between special and universal providence may be illustrated as follows: an actuality that is produced or maintained by a system of causation different from that governing all other existence is described as subject to special providence; an actuality governed by the same causation as all other existence is subject to universal providence. The concept of special providence appears to be coherent only within a system of metaphenomenal providence, and is usually associated with a theistic theology. The position is widely affirmed by religions of the Jewish religious complex that Jews come under the aegis of a special providence, which generally is based on the rationale that Jews are the chosen and covenanted people of Yahveh, God of the universe, by virtue of which they enjoy an extraordinary relation to him entailing a unique destiny. This destiny has been understood in various ways, from earthly to heavenly survival, and from mundane to spiritual supremacy. A notable exception to the general agreement that a special providence rules Jewish existence is the medieval philosophic tradition, where the notion is widespread (although frequently left implicit and unstated) that the Jews are subject to universal providence together with all other peoples and societies. Yet interestingly enough, Judah ha-Levi, who was knowledgeable in philosophic thought, gives in his *Kuzari* perhaps the most striking and extreme formulation of the view that Jews enjoy a special providence, maintaining that even the nature of the being of the Jew is qualitatively superior to that of all other humans.

Static and Dynamic Providence

The final distinction is that between static and dynamic providence. Static providence is the concept that the causal ground is constant and unchanging, so that if the ground ever produces or maintains an actuality, it will always continue to do so; or should an action or set of actions by humans ever have served to realize or preserve existence, they likewise will always continue to do so. Dynamic providence, on the other hand, is the concept that the causal ground is subject to change, so that it is not necessarily the case that the ground, having produced or maintained some actuality, will always continue to do so—or that some action or actions by humans, having in the past realized or preserved existence, will thus always continue to be efficacious.

In the Jewish religious complex, the view has been virtually universal that the providence governing Jewish existence is static. Moreover, in the various theologies of Jewish survival that perennial crises of existence have prompted, the concept of static providence has been repeatedly employed as the basis for inaction or reaction in dealing with these crises. The argument is given either that inasmuch as the causal ground has favored the generation or preservation of Jewish existence in the past, and this ground (according to static providence) is unchanging, it will continue to do so in the future, and Jewish survival without furthur effort is assured; or, inasmuch as certain actions (beliefs, rituals, and the like) have served to bring forth Jewish existence from the causal ground in the past, and this ground (according to static providence) is unchanging, then the same actions will continue to bring forth Jewish existence from the ground in the future, and without change or innovation Jewish survival is assured. From the efforts of the early Reform Jews to fashion a Judaism relevant to their time, it might appear that they subscribed to a notion of dynamic providence.[9] In reality, this is not the case. These Reformers did not fathom the radical nature of the changes they introduced; neither did they understand their efforts as meeting the demands of a changing providence. Their reformation was taken as nonessential rather than essential, as removing the incrustation of the ages from the essence of a fixed Judaism rather than introducing another new system into the flux of the Jewish religious complex.[10]

The categories of providence relating to Jewish existence having been detailed, it is clear that the Jewish religious complex is of no one mind regarding a theology of Jewish survival. There is no single theology of Jewish survival as there is no single Jewish theology. Owing to its pluralistic composition, therefore, the complex is necessarily limited to a heuristic function, clarifying issues and pointing to the options before us. Thus by indirection, in not presenting one choice, the past calls us to act in freedom, to choices that are ultimately our own. The theology of Jewish survival I find convincing is based upon the concept of hylotheism presented earlier.[11]

A Hylotheistic Theology of Jewish Survival

First, it appears to be clearly the case that the existence of the Jewish religious complex is subject to phenomenal providence alone. Three reasons may be given for rejecting the concept of metaphenomenal providence: the complete lack of acceptable evidence that any metaphenomenal event has ever occurred in the past, the complete inability to point to a metaphenomenal event in the present, and the refutation of all proofs for theistic absolutism. The primary records reporting metaphenomenal occurrences in relation to Jewish existence are those appearing in the Bible and Talmud, works whose historical accuracy is rejected by critical scholarship.[12] No record of a metaphenomenal event is reported in the annals of critically reliable history. Similarly, no metaphenomenal event can be pointed to in the present. All events in relation to modern Jewry, such as the Holocaust or the establishment of the state of Israel, are reducible to phenomenal causation, and are actually incoherent except in terms of such causation.[13] Metaphenomenal interpretations placed upon such events may have emotive and imaginative value, but cannot be shown to have any basis in fact. Nevertheless, despite the absence of evidence that there has ever been an instance of metaphenomenal providence, belief in the possibility of such an occurrence in the future would be reasonable if theistic absolutism could be shown objectively to be true, since theistic absolutism entails the divine capacity for metaphenomenal acts. Hence the refutation in modern philosophy and theology of all attempts to establish theistic absolutism removes the last reasonable or coherent basis for belief in a metaphenomenal providence.[14] In sum, then, when Jews have gone to the auto-da-fé or concentration camps, they have done so owing to the collapse of bankrupt economies and the primitiveness of a human species evolved from earlier animal forms; and when Jews find existence assured, it is because they and humankind generally have made successful use of the phenomenal order, economies are productive, political institutions are stable, and science is flourishing.

Second, the existence of the Jewish religious complex is subject to conditional providence alone. Absolute providence is rejected for reasons similar to those given above for the rejection of metaphenomenal providence: the absence of evidence, the refutation of theistic absolutism, and the refutation of metaphenomenal providence itself. In every instance of reliably reported history, and more important, in present living experience, Jews have succeeded in surviving only upon meeting phenomenal conditions of existence. Where they have not, whether in ancient Israel or Nazi Germany, they have been decimated or annihilated. It can be argued that absolute providence extends to the total community of Jews, so that while there are any Jews alive at all the concept cannot be disproved. The answer is that those Jews who have survived can be shown to have lived under circumstances that met the phenomenal conditions of existence. The point then is: when Jews have met the phenomenal conditions of existence (after having either met metaphenomenal requirements or not), they have survived; when Jews have not met the phenomenal conditions of existence (after having either met metaphenomenal requirements or not), they have perished. Moreover, it is inconsistent to maintain, on one hand, that absolute providence extends to a collectivity, but, on the other, that the individuals constituting the collectivity are left to conditional providence or to chance. The refutation of theistic absolutism and metaphenomenal providence is also fatal to the concept of absolute providence, in that they provide the only plausible ground for the latter. It should be emphasized that inasmuch as metaphenomenal providence is refuted, the conditions of existence that must be met are those of phenomenal providence.

Third, no distinction is to be drawn between individual and general providence; the causal ground governing the Jewish individual and the Jewish collectivity is the same. The denial of the distinction between individual and general providence follows from the foregoing discussion. With the rejection of metaphenomenal providence, any basis for distinction between individual and general providence is set aside. Hence the individual and the collectivity are both necessarily subject to the same causal principles, those constituting phenomenal providence. As for the possibility that the distinction between the providence of the individual and the collectivity is that one is eternal and the other is not, this is dismissed by the refutation of eternal providence which follows.

Fourth, the existence of the Jewish religious complex is subject to temporal providence alone. Primarily, the reason for the rejection of eternal providence is that there is simply no evidence to justify its acceptance. We have no experience of any actuality, whether an individual or a collectivity, maintaining itself for more than a limited period of time. All individuals who have lived either have died, or by inductive reasoning, can be said will die. Regarding collectivities, critical study of the past reveals that no political state, social institution, or religious community that exists today was present at the dawn of history, and those that were present have long since perished. Furthermore, the evidence from the physical sciences refutes the belief of medievals like Maimonides that the heavens and earthly species are eternal; instead, such evidence strongly supports the notion that galaxies and species arise and die, and that the cosmos itself undergoes radical, evolutionary change. The Jewish religious complex perhaps serves best to illustrate the truth of temporal providence in human affairs: no purported revelation, no God concept, no ritual, and no worship subscribed to in the earliest Jewish systems is adhered to today. Even the names Jew and Judaism are emergents that were unknown to the first persons today called Jews. The Jewish religious process has survived not as the same actuality, but as a complex of different religions enjoying constant creativity and novelty.

Fifth, the existence of the Jewish religious complex is subject to universal providence alone. No evidence can be brought to substantiate a special providence for Jews. The unusual experiences of Jews through history are coherently explained not by reference to a special causal ground, but by a universal ground acting on people who, owing to phenomenal causation, had developed differently. To be sure, the present, concrete life of Jews is adequately explained by universal providence alone. Moreover, with the refutation of metaphenomenal providence, no competent theoretical basis for the concept of special providence can be found, since in the phenomenal order all persons and communities are subject to the same providence.

Sixth, the existence of the Jewish religious complex is subject to dynamic providence alone. The categories of static and dynamic providence stand in close relation to those of eternal and temporal providence, but they differ in the following way. The point at issue between eternal and temporal providence is whether the causal ground provides any actuality with eternal existence, whereas the issue between static and dynamic providence is whether the causal ground is in constant flux and so can neither preserve the same actuality nor reproduce essentially the same actuality at a new time.[15] The view of dynamic providence is that the causal ground is forever changing, and as the ground changes so can it produce only novel effects or actualities, and so must the causes that can produce existence from the ground be novel as well. The view of dynamic providence is compelling because we find nothing in experience that is lasting or even unchanging. From subatomic particles and human history to the great galaxies and the universe itself, novelty and death are the pervasive characteristics of being. Static providence simply plays no role in existence, and it can be discarded as a superfluous or meaningless concept whose roots are in fantasy not reality. Certainly the Jewish religious complex displays every evidence of being governed by a dynamic providence. The actuality every Jewish system has sought to realize from the ground of existence is the state of the human being called soteria.[16] Yet no one system has been able to prescribe a course of action, whether of belief or observance, that has been efficacious for all Jews in every place and in every age. The disparate religious systems of the Jewish religious complex have ultimately arisen in response to the demand of a fluxing ground that requires novel responses in order to produce soteria. These novel religious systems in turn are the reason for the survival of the Jewish religious complex, since they alone can realize the possibilities of soteria from a dynamic ground, and the power to realize soteria is the ultimate *raison d'être* for every religious system. If the power to effect soteria is lost, there is no further justification for the survival of the Jewish religious complex, and little reason to believe it will survive.

Hylotheism

One last point remains to be made regarding the providence that governs Jewish existence. The providence, or causal ground, that governs Jewish existence is, in the author's view, nothing other than the hylotheistic Godhead, namely, the enduring possibility of being.[17] It is from the enduring possibility of being that all existence is realized; and the characteristics of providence as phenomenal, conditional, temporal, universal, and dynamic flow directly from the Godhead itself. As God, the causal ground is ultimate; there are no appeals beyond it for existence.

The Future and Polydoxy

The aforestated theology of Jewish survival, applied to the present situation of the Jewish religious complex, proposes the following thesis. Evidence of decline of the Jewish religious complex is everywhere visible. These are not superficial symptoms, but point to a grave situation, a crisis of existence deeper than any other in Jewish religious history. We live in a period of radical movement within the Godhead relative to humankind. This period is unlike any heretofore experienced by the Jewish religious complex. And as the Godhead undergoes fundamental change, so do the conditions of existence and soteria required of humankind generally and of religious communities in particular. The survival of a religion subject to phenomenal providence is dependent upon human persons, who, owing to their finity, are bound to economy in their existence. They cannot sustain for long the burden of that which does not respond to their essential soterial needs. The economic system that does not provide food is destroyed, the political institution that does not govern is overthrown, the religion irrelevant to the human's primary concern of soteria is discarded.[18] The present manifest of the Jewish religious complex, excepting Polydox Judaism, does not meet the test of relevance;[19] it is not grounded in the general intellectual, moral, and cultural climate of our time. Instead, again aside from Polydox Judaism, the manifest of the Jewish religious complex has become increasingly incredible, and so is largely impotent to realize the possibilities of soteria residing in the Godhead.

No panacea exists to resolve the present situation of the Jewish religious complex. To produce a *deus ex machina* would be a mockery. The problem is rooted in the radical becoming of the Godhead, and allows for no sure or simple solution. Yet steps can be taken that will provide a prologue to definitive action. First, and perhaps above all, Jews must become aware of the reality and shock of impending annihilation. The real nature of this threat should not be difficult to recognize in our time, which bears daily witness to the extinction of the familiar. Moreover, the polydox potentialities of the Jewish religious complex should be realized. Not only would this concretize freedom, the highest ideal possible to the modern religious community, but it would also make possible the creativity and experimentation necessary to meet the conditions of a radical and unknown future. In addition, the Jewish religious complex must make widely available deanthropomorphized and demythologized options of belief and observance. The present manifest is by and large impotent, and is a major reason for the present widespread alienation and estrangement of Jews from the Jewish religious complex. Finally, the educational ideal of the Jewish religious complex should become that of polydoxy, moving away from endoctrining instruction in theistic absolutism and metaphenomenal providence to education in the soterial, ethical, and theological choices of an open religion. Members of the Jewish religious complex, young and old, will thus be called to develop the courage to respond creatively to the challenges of freedom and novelty, and to find soteria in the face of the angst they produce.

Notes

1. The name *Jew* is not used here to designate persons for whom the name has primarily ethnic or political significance. In the author's view the religious significance of the name Jew is its fundamental value. Use of the

term Jew as a name with religious significance includes notably the function of the name Jew as an ontal symbol. See above, pp. 166 f.

2. The term *Judaism* is often used to refer to the variety of religions Jews have adhered to over the millennia. Unfortunately, the term is misleading in that it makes it seem that Jews have subscribed to one religion in the course of their history when, in fact, they have subscribed to many, such as Sadducean Judaism, Pharisaic Judaism, Maimonidean Judaism, Reform Judaism, and so forth. The continuing creation of religions (i.e., responses to the conflict of finitude) by the Jews is called by the author the *Jewish religious process*. See above, p. 75.

3. Maimonides has already framed the meaning of providence in this way. See the *Guide of the Perplexed*, III, 17. See my "Maimonides' Concepts of Providence and Theodicy," *Hebrew Union College Annual*, XLIII (1972), pp. 177-193.

4. *Loc. cit.* See also my "Maimonides' Concepts of Providence and Theodicy."

5. As in Amos and the preexilic prophets generally.

6. As in Pharisaism or its contemporary counterpart, Orthodox Judaism.

7. I.e., the person either dies in accordance with the phenomenal order, or attains resurrection or immortality, which requires intervention of the metaphenomenal order.

8. Whether complete nonexistence or nonexistence for all significant purposes, as, e.g., existence in Sheol is nonexistence for all significant purposes inasmuch as those who are there are mere shadows without knowledge or feeling.

9. As, e.g., from a notion such as "progressive revelation."

10. It might be added that by the lack of awareness that they were attempting to respond to a dynamic providence, the early Reformers bequeathed neither a significant understanding of the need for continuing change in the Jewish religious complex, nor a productive theoretical apparatus that would provide smoothly for future reformations past their own.

11. See above pp. 176 ff.

12. Metaphenomenal occurrences in relation to Jewish existence are specified because Jewish existence is the subject. It should be pointed out that no critically reliable evidence exists that metaphenomenal events have occurred to any other people or religious group.

13. I.e., theologically incoherent. No theodicy has shown that a concept of deity such as theistic absolutism, which describes a deity capable of metaphenomenal acts and also worthy of worship, is reconcilable with an evil such as the Holocaust.

14. No serious evidence is put forth at the present time for miracle-working deities other than theistic absolutism, such as, e.g., the gods of Greek mythology.

15. Accordingly, if the concept of dynamic providence is true, temporal

providence is necessarily true; but if static providence is true, either eternal or temporal providence is true.

16. See above, p. 63.
17. See above, n. 11.
18. See above, pp. 75 f.
19. By *manifest* is meant the readily visible aspects of a religious movement, such as the liturgy, ceremonial structure, mode of instructional organization (free or authoritarian), and educational system.

Index

Jew (Judaism); Reform Jewish Community, analogues of; universal polydoxies
angst, 62
annihilation: of meaning of existence, 62; of the actual, 176; reality for Jews of, 198
anti-Semitism, 104, 130n.61, 145
Aquinas, Saint Thomas, 162
Aristotle: and theology, 159; cosmological argument by, 113; *Metaphysics*, 162; theology of, 162
asoteria: and ontal decision, 72-76; definition of, 63; from intense conflict, 71
asoterial agony, 69
atheonomatism, 58
"atom," 181n.5
atonement, 115, 140
authentic religion, 69, 71-72; without theistic absolutism, 57-58
authentic response: based on reality, 168; in Polydox Judaism, 167-168; knowledge of self and, 175
authenticity, 13
authoritarian prophetic figures, 28
authoritarian religion: based on ratio-moral authority principle, 122; definition of, 24; interpersonal structure of, 11; referred to as Orthodox, 24. *See also* Absolute Authority Principle; orthodox religion
authoritarian religious communities: based on ratio-moral authority principle, 122; beliefs and practices of, 24; belief in Absolute Authority Principle of, 24; definition of, 24; leadership of, 24, 45. *See also* orthodox communities
authoritative revelation, 161. *See also* revelation, verbal
authority: as determinor of catego-

ries of religion, 125; by power, 14-15; by right, 14-15; community's concept of, 124-125; conditional, 16, 29, 31n.29; definition of, 13, 14; delegation of, by theistic god, 17, 122; in Catholicism, 151; in Polydox community, 28-29; in Reform Judaism and analogues, 13-19, 123; morality of, 16-18, 122, 125; rational, 122; reasons for possession of, 14; right to, 16-18, 23, 41, 122; and subjective theology, 162. *See also* absolute authority; authority, self
authority, self: as organizational principle of religious community, 25; assured through Freedom Covenant, 40; communal relationship and, 24; exercise of, 26; in polydoxy, 28-29; modernist Judaism and, 151; right to Freedom Covenant, 34; right to, 16, 23, 25, 26, 29; right to, without verbal revelation, 41; transfer of, 16, 29. *See also* autonomy
authority of Pope, 35
autonomy: affirmed by liberal religions, 40; affirmed by Polydox Judaism, 167; affirmed by Polydoxy, 155; as religious self-authority, 25, 155; as ultimate right, 25; framed as Freedom Covenant, 40; of each Polydoxian, 45; opposed by Pentateuch, 126n.11; right of members of Reform community and its analogues, 23; surrendered to orthodox leaders, 45; violated through endoctrining, 46. *See also* authority, self

baptism, 140
being, 175-177, 180
belief(s): actions and, 16; ambiguous

34, 40-42; principles of, 36; rejection of, in Polydoxy, 41, 157; supernatural, 37
dogmatic definition, expectation of, 157
drug addiction, 69
dynamic meaning, 166-168
dynamic providence, 191, 196
dynamic theology, 167-168
dyssoteria: definition of, 63; ontal decision and, 73; widespread, 68, 73
dyssoterial agony, 69

Ecclesiastes, 74, 75
economic conditions challenging belief in Orthodox Judaism, 102-104
ecumenism, 135-152
education: definition of, 45-46; in polydox community, 45-46, 76; in soterial, ethical, theological choices, 198; Jewish, pre-nineteenth century, 107, 109; necessary for finite response, 76; propaganda in theistic absolutism and, 56, 198; vs. endoctrining, 45-46, 198
educational ideal, 198
egotheistic deity, 64
emergent religion(s): definition of, 134n.108; matrix religions and, 124
emotion(s): as base of religious beliefs, 22; finite, 59
empirical experience (as understood by science), 36, 39
empirical verifiability, 163, 175
empiricism, 36, 39, 148
endoctrining: as opposite of education, 46; definition of, 46; in concept of one Jewish religion, 80; instruction, 198; prohibited by

Freedom Covenant, 46
enduring possibility of being, 175-176; accounts for problem of evil, 179-180; correlative of being, 177; world and, 177. See also hylotheism
Enoch Arden law, 107
essence: of Judaism, 122-123; of polydoxy, 47, 52n.31; of Reform, 13; of religion, 52n.31, 160; of theistic absolutistic religions, 57
essential(s): definition of, 41; for Polydox Jews, 47
essential beliefs and practices: as religion, 96; as criterion for determining different religions, 95-98; definition of, 41, 96-97; identical, 98; nonidentical, 98; of different religions, 98; of Orthodox Judaism, 94, 99, 108-109, 112, 117-119; of Reform Judaism, 117-119; of same religion, 98; rejection of, 108-117. See also essentials
essential Polydox Judaism, 47
essential Reform Judaism, 49
estrangement, 198
eternal providence, 189
Ethical Cultural Movement, 35-36
ethics of hypothetical necessity, 178-179
ethnicism, 123
evidence: characteristic of our age regarding, 170; classes of, 83-86; criticism of biblical, 69; faith and, 83; fallible, in Polydox Judaism, 167; for Christianity, Jesus, and New Testament, 67; for covenant with Hebrews, 85; for existence of Yahveh, 85; for human origin of sacred books, 111, 112; for infallible communication of commandments, 93-95; for infinite relational response, 67-68; for

negative moods, 62, 63

negative theology, 164, 180-181

New Testament: as derivation of view of Jewish religion, 81; Bible and, 30n.15, 81; divine status of, 35, 67-68; document for Revelation Authority Argument, 67; special status of, 35; supernatural revelation and, 81. *See also* Revelation Authority Argument

New Testament Christian(s), 125n.7

New Testament Christianity: alternative to, 82; conditions affecting belief in, 100; credibility of, 81; definition of, 125n.7

nineteenth-century challenges to belief in Orthodox Judaism: cultural, 106-108; economic, 102-104; intellectual, 108-117; political, 100-102; social, 104-106

nonessential beliefs: definition of, 41; of religion, 41, 96; optional, 96; polydoxy and, 45, 48

nonevidential faith, 83, 87, 91

neurosis, 68

Noah, author of, 181

nothing, 176

"now existent," 167, 182n.19

objective evidence: as basis of true religion, 174; definition of, 84-85, 163; empirical verifiability of, 175; of revelation, 170; pre-nineteenth-century Jewish systems and, 91-92; reality reference for God based on, 174; repeatable, 84-85, 163; theology, 174; theology based on, 163; theories of truth and, 175; unrepeatable, 84, 126n.18, 163

obsolete religion, 75

Old Testament, 81-82. *See also* Bible

omnipotence, desire for, 61

ontal: change, 63; decision, 47-48, 63, 65-66, 73; decision as resolver of pain and conflict, 65-66, 178; structure, 63-65, 72; symbol, 166-168, 175-176; symbol for word "Christian," 52n.33, 182; symbol for word "Jew," 52n.33, 166-167, 182

ontological argument, 84, 113, 114

Ontos, 166

opinions, in polydoxy, 160

oral law. *See* Talmud

organized religion: decline of, 55; definition of religion in, 55-58; future of, 57. *See also* Western religious institutions

original sin. *See* sin

Orthodox ceremonial calendar, 103, 106

Orthodox Christians, 30n.15

Orthodox communities: Absolute Authority Principle and, 24; based on ratio-moral authority principle, 122; creed of, 45; endoctrination in, 46; establishment of, 44; form of, 24, 122; leadership of, 45; obligatory observances of, 45. *See also* theistic absolutistic religions

Orthodox Covenant, 120, 121

Orthodox Jewish Cognate Complex, 72, 81-83, 120

Orthodox Judaism: as form of theology, 114, 161; as infinite relational response religion, 65-68; beliefs of, 94-95, 96, 99-100, 118-119; compared with Pharisaism, 93, 97-98, 199n.6; compared with Reform Judaism, 60, 118-119; conditions affecting belief in, 100-117; evidence for belief in, 66-67, 90-91; founding of community, 44; in political and social

al response religion and, 66; in Polydoxy, 164; Mosaic, 67, 95, 98, 99-102, 115, 118-120; natural, 20, 22; nature of, 125; obligatory, 18-19; Orthodox Judaism and, 44, 45, 93; ratio-moral authority principle of, 122, 125; Reform Judaism and, 21-23, 118-121; rejection of infallible, 21-23, 35, 108-110, 111-113, 122-123, 148, 161-162, 174, 178; right to reject, 21; Sinaitic, 21, 84, 92-93, 118, 120; theistic deity and, 18, 20, 56, 118, 122; theology based on, 161-162; verbal, 18, 21, 45, 99, 161. *See also* Revelation Authority Argument

Revelation Authority Argument: acceptance of, 18; authority over others in, 22; definition of, 16-18; justified by ratio-moral authority principle, 122; moral right to absolute authority in, 16-17; rejection of, 21-23, 26, 110-112; view of revelation necessary to sustain, 18-23. *See also* revelation

Roman Catholicism: as dixit evidence religion, 90; as infinite relational response religion, 65; as form of theology, 161; as New Testament Christianity, 82; community founded by Jesus, 44; conditions affecting belief in, 100-117, 124; essential beliefs of, 96; infallible revelation in, 67; Jews and, 81, 137-152; supernatural dogmas of, 37; theistic deity in, 114; Trinity in, 96, 98. *See also* Christianity; Fundamentalist Protestantism; Sunni Islam; Orthodox Judaism; Western world religion

Saadiah, 162

sabbath: as a state of being, 30n.12; commandments regarding, rejected by Conservatism, 123; divine imperative for, 20; human in origin, 20; literal observance of, 18, 103

Sadducaic Judaism: afterlife in, 74, 93; as finite response religion, 74-75; as sacrificial cult of Temple, 93; basis of, 93; in New Testament, 125n.6; Moses and Pentateuch in, 93; part of religious Jewish complex, 199n.2

salvation: brought by obedience to the Torah, 147; key to, 82; Modernist Judaism and, 148; obstacles to, 140; supernatural, 150. *See also* soteria

same religions, 97

science(s): alternative method for dealing with world problems, 115; dogma of, 39; as faith-after-inquiry, 109; as threat to orthodox belief, 115-116; naturalism and, 116; on religious belief, 39; physical and social, 84-109; technology in nineteenth century and, 115; vs. supernatural providence, 116

scientific method, 110. *See also* higher criticism

scripture: critical and objective study of, 174; fallible, 13-15, 174; referring to Bible (Jewish), 14, 21; referring to Old Testament (Christian), 14; religion without, 14. *See also* documents supporting Revelation Authority Argument

self: access to, 66; knowledge of, 175. *See also* human person

selfa (self-data), 85, 175-176

self-authority. *See* authority, self;

autonomy self-data, 85, 175-176
semantic impediments to autonomy, 55-57, 155-159
sensa (sense-data), 175-176
sexism, 126n.11
sin: in orthodox Judaism, 94-95; original, 140
Sinaitic revelation. *See* revelation; Covenant, Sinaitic
social conditions challenging belief in Orthodox Judaism, 104-105
solitary religion, 36
soteria: as essence of finite response, 76; as function of religion, 63, 75; as right in polydoxy, 73; conditions for, 197; definition of, 63, 149; in face of anxiety, 198; in finite response religions, 70-72; in infinite response religions, 65-68; integration of consciousness and will, 70; loss of power to effect, 196; modernist view of, 149; natural revelation and, 20; obsolete religion and, 75; obstacle to, 149; ontal decision required for, 72; possibilities residing in Godhead, 198; power to realize, 196; proper claim of religious community, 76; purpose of Jewish religious complex, 75, 196; search for, 20; ultimate meaningful existence, 70-72
special providence: affirmed by religions of Jewish religious complex, 190; associated with theistic theology, 190; definition of, 190; no evidence for, 195; of Orthodox Covenant, 92
Spinoza, Baruch: *Ethics,* 162; excommunication of, 131n.69; pantheistic absolutism of, 179; philosophy of, 131n.69; problem of evil, 179; rationalism of, 51n.23;

theology based on certain natural knowledge, 162; use of word "God," 158
starvation, 115
State of Israel, 125n.5, 193
static: meaning, 167; providence, 191, 192; rule, 163-164; use of terms, 163
subjective evidence, 85-86; theology based on, 162-163
subjective evidence theology: apprehension of a "presence," 171; consistent with Polydox Judaism, 173-174; criterion for determining truth, 162, 171-174; critique of, 171-172; definition of, 162; relationship to theistic absolutism, 170-171
substantive will, 72
suicide, 68-69
Sunni Islam: Allah as God in, 97-98; as dixit evidence religion, 90; as infinite relational response religion, 65; conditions affecting belief in, 100-117, 124; essential beliefs of, 96; evidence for belief in, 66-67; expectations of Jews by, 82; founding of community, 44, 73; Mohammed and, 44, 67; theistic deity in, 114. *See also* Christianity; Fundamentalist Protestantism; Orthodox Judaism; Roman Catholicism; Western world religion
supernatural: activity by theistic God, 18-20; communication with theistic God, 86; covenant, 120-121; deity, 39, 76; dogmas, 37, 40; providence, 115, 117, 187; religion, 116, 123; subjective evidence, 85-86
surd evil, 173
survival: individual, 115; religious,